SEX DISCRIMINATION AND HARASSMENT

LEGAL DEVELOPMENTS AND PROPOSALS

LAWS AND LEGISLATION

Additional books in this series can be found on Nova's website
under the Series tab.

Additional e-books in this series can be found on Nova's website
under the e-book tab.

LAWS AND LEGISLATION

SEX DISCRIMINATION AND HARASSMENT

LEGAL DEVELOPMENTS AND PROPOSALS

HERBERT D. ANDREWS
AND
SEAN O. SPENCER
EDITORS

publishers
New York

For permission to use material from this book please contact us:
Telephone 631-231-7269; Fax 631-231-8175
Web Site: http://www.novapublishers.com

NOTICE TO THE READER

The Publisher has taken reasonable care in the preparation of this book, but makes no expressed or implied warranty of any kind and assumes no responsibility for any errors or omissions. No liability is assumed for incidental or consequential damages in connection with or arising out of information contained in this book. The Publisher shall not be liable for any special, consequential, or exemplary damages resulting, in whole or in part, from the readers' use of, or reliance upon, this material. Any parts of this book based on government reports are so indicated and copyright is claimed for those parts to the extent applicable to compilations of such works.

Independent verification should be sought for any data, advice or recommendations contained in this book. In addition, no responsibility is assumed by the publisher for any injury and/or damage to persons or property arising from any methods, products, instructions, ideas or otherwise contained in this publication.

This publication is designed to provide accurate and authoritative information with regard to the subject matter covered herein. It is sold with the clear understanding that the Publisher is not engaged in rendering legal or any other professional services. If legal or any other expert assistance is required, the services of a competent person should be sought. FROM A DECLARATION OF PARTICIPANTS JOINTLY ADOPTED BY A COMMITTEE OF THE AMERICAN BAR ASSOCIATION AND A COMMITTEE OF PUBLISHERS.

Additional color graphics may be available in the e-book version of this book.

Library of Congress Cataloging-in-Publication Data

ISBN 978-1-62257-466-7

Published by Nova Science Publishers, Inc. † New York

CONTENTS

PREFACE

This book examines the legal developments and proposals concerning sexual discrimination and sexual harassment in federal law. Gender-based discrimination, sexual harassment, and violence against women in the workplace, schools, and society at large are continuing topics of legislative and judicial concern. Legal doctrines condemning the extortion of sexual favors as a condition of employment of job advancement and other sexually offensive workplace behaviors resulting in a "hostile environment" have evolved from judicial decisions under Title VII of the 1964 Civil Rights Act and other federal equal employment opportunity laws. In recent years, the U.S. Supreme Court has addressed a range of sexual harassment issues, from the legality of same-sex harassment to the vicarious liability of employers and local school districts for monetary damages as a result of harassment by supervisors and teachers. These and other significant Supreme Court cases regarding sexual harassment and violence against women are also discussed.

Chapter 1 – Gender-based discrimination, sexual harassment, and violence against women in the workplace, schools, and society at large are continuing topics of legislative and judicial concern.

Legal doctrines condemning the extortion of sexual favors as a condition of employment or job advancement and other sexually offensive workplace behaviors resulting in a "hostile environment" have evolved from judicial decisions under Title VII of the 1964 Civil Rights Act and other federal equal employment opportunity laws. The earlier judicial focus on economic detriment or *quid pro quo* harassment—that is, making submission to sexual demands a condition of job benefits—has largely given way to Title VII claims alleging harassment that creates an "intimidating, hostile, or offensive

environment." Under Title IX of the Education Amendments of 1972, victims
of sexual harassment that occurs in a public school setting may make similar
quid pro quo or hostile environment claims.

Chapter 2 – In its sex discrimination decisions, the United States Supreme
Court not only has defined the applicability of the equal protection guarantees
of the Constitution and the nondiscriminatory policies of federal statutes, but
also has rejected the use of gender stereotypes and has continued to recognize
the discriminatory effect of gender hostility in the workplace and in schools.
This report focuses on sex discrimination challenges based on: the equal
protection guarantees of the Fourteenth and Fifth Amendments; the prohibition
against employment discrimination contained in Title VII of the Civil Rights
Act of 1964; and the prohibition against sex discrimination in education
contained in Title IX of the Education Amendments of 1972. Although this
report focuses on recent legal developments in each of these areas, this report
also provides historical context by discussing selected landmark sex
discrimination cases.

Despite the fact that the Court's analysis of sex discrimination challenges
under the Constitution differs from its analysis of sex discrimination under the
two federal statutes discussed in this report, it is apparent that the Court is
willing to refine its standards of review under both schemes to accommodate
the novel claims presented by these cases. The Court's decisions in cases
involving Title VII and Title IX are particularly noteworthy because they
illustrate the Court's recognition of sexual harassment in both the workplace
and the classroom.

During the recent 2010-2011 term, the Court issued rulings in two high-
profile cases involving claims of sex discrimination in employment. In
Thompson v. North American Stainless, which involved a retaliation claim by
a man who was fired three weeks after his then-fiancée filed a sex discrimination complaint, the Court determined that Title VII of the Civil Rights Act
protects third parties who have not personally engaged in protected activity
from retaliation by employers. In *Wal-Mart Store v. Dukes*, the Court rejected
class action status for current and former female Wal-Mart employees who
allege that the company has engaged in discrimination regarding pay and
promotions.

Chapter 3 – Introduced in various incarnations in every congressional
session since the 103rd Congress, the proposed Employment Non-Discrimination Act (ENDA; H.R. 1397/S. 811) would prohibit discrimination based on

an individual's actual or perceived sexual orientation or gender identity by public and private employers in hiring, discharge, compensation, and other terms and conditions of employment. The stated purpose of the legislation is "to address the history and widespread pattern of discrimination on the basis of sexual orientation or gender identity by private sector employers and local, State, and Federal Government employers," as well as to provide effective remedies for such discrimination. Patterned on Title VII of the Civil Rights Act of 1964, the act would be enforced by the Equal Employment Opportunity Commission (EEOC).

Chapter 4 – The term "pay equity" originates from the fact that women as a group are paid less than men. In recent years, for example, women with a strong commitment to the workforce earned about 77 to 80 cents for every dollar earned by men. As women's earnings as a percentage of men's earnings have narrowed by less than 20 percentage points over the past 40-plus years, some members of the public policy community have argued that current anti-discrimination laws should be strengthened and that additional measures should be enacted. Others, in contrast, believe that further government intervention is unnecessary because the gender wage gap will narrow on its own as women's labor market qualifications continue to more closely resemble those of men.

The Equal Pay Act (EPA), which amends the Fair Labor Standards Act (FLSA), prohibits covered employers from paying lower wages to female employees than male employees for "equal work" on jobs requiring "equal skill, effort, and responsibility" and performed "under similar working conditions" at the same location. The FLSA exempts some jobs (e.g., hotel service workers) from EPA coverage, and the EPA makes exceptions for wage differentials based on merit or seniority systems, systems that measure earnings by "quality or quantity" of production, or "any factor other than sex." The "equal work" standard embodies a middle ground between demanding that two jobs either be exactly alike or that they merely be comparable. The test applied by the courts focuses on job similarity and whether, given all the circumstances, they require substantially the same skill, effort, and responsibility. The EPA may be enforced by the government, or individual complainants, in civil actions for wages unlawfully withheld and liquidated damages for willful violations. In addition, Title VII of the 1964 Civil Rights Act provides for the awarding of compensatory and punitive damages to victims of "intentional" wage discrimination, subject to caps on the employer's monetary liability.

The issue of pay equity has attracted substantial attention in recent Congresses. A number of measures, including bills that would provide additional remedies, mandate "equal pay for equivalent jobs," or require studies on pay inequity, have been introduced in each of the last several congressional sessions. These bills include the Paycheck Fairness Act (H.R. 1519/S. 3220) and the Fair Pay Act (H.R. 1493/S. 788). Meanwhile, in *Wal-Mart Stores v. Dukes*, the Supreme Court recently rejected class action status for current and former female Wal-Mart employees who allege that the company has engaged in pay discrimination.

Chapter 5 – Enacted nearly four decades ago, Title IX of the Education Amendments of 1972 prohibits discrimination on the basis of sex in federally funded education programs or activities. Although the Title IX regulations bar recipients of federal financial assistance from discriminating on the basis of sex in a wide range of educational programs or activities, such as student admissions, scholarships, and access to courses, the statute is perhaps best known for prohibiting sex discrimination in intercollegiate athletics.

Indeed, the provisions regarding athletics have proved to be one of the more controversial aspects of Title IX. At the center of the debate is a three-part test that the Department of Education (ED) uses to determine whether institutions are providing nondiscriminatory athletic participation opportunities for both male and female students. Proponents of the existing regulations point to the dramatic increases in the number of female athletes in elementary and secondary school, college, and beyond as the ultimate indicator of the statute's success in breaking down barriers against women in sports. In contrast, opponents contend that the Title IX regulations unfairly impose quotas on collegiate sports and force universities to cut men's teams in order to remain in compliance. Critics further argue that the decline in certain men's sports, such as wrestling, is a direct result of Title IX's emphasis on proportionality in men's and women's college sports.

In 2002, ED appointed a commission to study Title IX and to recommend whether or not the athletics provisions should be revised. The Commission on Opportunity in Athletics delivered its final report to the Secretary of Education in 2003. In response, ED issued new guidance in 2003 and 2005 that clarified Title IX policy and the use of the three-part test.

This CRS report provides an overview of Title IX in general and the intercollegiate athletics regulations in particular, as well as a summary of the commission's report and ED's response and a discussion of legal challenges to the regulations and to the three-part test.

Chapter 6 – Under Title IX of the Education Amendments of 1972, which prohibits sex discrimination in federally funded education programs or activities, school districts have long been permitted to operate single-sex schools. In 2006, the Department of Education (ED) published Title IX regulations that, for the first time, authorized schools to establish single-sex classrooms as well. This report evaluates the regulations in light of statutory requirements under Title IX and the Equal Educational Opportunities Act (EEOA) and in consideration of constitutional equal protection requirements.

In: Sex Discrimination and Harassment   ISBN 978-1-62257-466-7
Editors: H. Andrews and S. Spencer   © 2012 Nova Science Publishers, Inc.

Chapter 1

SEXUAL HARASSMENT: DEVELOPMENTS IN FEDERAL LAW[*]

Jody Feder

SUMMARY

Gender-based discrimination, sexual harassment, and violence against women in the workplace, schools, and society at large are continuing topics of legislative and judicial concern.

Legal doctrines condemning the extortion of sexual favors as a condition of employment or job advancement and other sexually offensive workplace behaviors resulting in a "hostile environment" have evolved from judicial decisions under Title VII of the 1964 Civil Rights Act and other federal equal employment opportunity laws. The earlier judicial focus on economic detriment or *quid pro quo* harassment—that is, making submission to sexual demands a condition of job benefits—has largely given way to Title VII claims alleging harassment that creates an "intimidating, hostile, or offensive environment." Under Title IX of the Education Amendments of 1972, victims of sexual harassment that occurs in a public school setting may make similar *quid pro quo* or hostile environment claims.

---

[*] This is an edited, reformatted and augmented version of Congressional Research Service, Publication No. RL33736, dated January 6, 2012.

INTRODUCTION

Gender-based discrimination, sexual harassment, and violence against women in the workplace, schools, and society at large are continuing topics of legislative and judicial concern. Legal doctrines condemning the extortion of sexual favors as a condition of employment or job advancement and other sexually offensive workplace behaviors resulting in a "hostile environment" have evolved from judicial decisions under Title VII of the 1964 Civil Rights Act and other federal equal employment opportunity laws.[1] The earlier judicial focus on economic detriment or *quid pro quo* harassment—that is, making submission to sexual demands a condition of job benefits—has largely given way to Title VII claims alleging harassment that creates an "intimidating, hostile, or offensive environment." Under Title IX of the Education Amendments of 1972,[2] victims of sexual harassment that occurs in a public school setting may make similar *quid pro quo* or hostile environment claims.

In recent years, the U.S. Supreme Court has addressed a range of sexual harassment issues, from the legality of same-sex harassment to the vicarious liability of employers and local school districts for monetary damages as the result of harassment by supervisors and teachers. These and other significant Supreme Court cases regarding sexual harassment and violence against women are discussed below.

FEDERAL EQUAL EMPLOYMENT OPPORTUNITY LAW

Title VII of the 1964 Civil Rights Act does not mention sexual harassment but makes it unlawful for employers with 15 or more employees to discriminate against any applicant or employee "because of ... sex."[3] Federal law on the subject is, therefore, largely a judicial creation, having evolved over four decades from federal court decisions and guidelines of the Equal Employment Opportunity Commission (EEOC) interpreting Title VII's sex discrimination prohibition.[4] Sexual harassment in federally assisted education programs is also prohibited by Title IX of the 1972 Education Amendments.[5] While Title VII and Title IX are the primary sources of federal sexual harassment law, relief from such conduct has also been sought, albeit less frequently, pursuant to §1983 of Title 42, the Federal Employees Liability Act, and the Equal Protection and Due Process Clauses of the U.S. Constitution.[6]

Two forms of sexual harassment have been recognized by the courts and EEOC administrative guidelines. The first, or *"quid pro quo"* harassment, occurs when submission to "unwelcome" sexual advances, propositions, or other conduct of a sexual nature is made an express or implied condition of employment, or where it is used as the basis of employment decisions affecting job status or tangible employment benefits. As its name suggests, this form of harassment involves actual or potential economic loss—such as termination, transfer, or adverse performance ratings—as a consequence of the employee's refusal to exchange sexual favors demanded by a supervisor or employer for employment benefits. The second form of actionable harassment consists of unwelcome sexual conduct that is of such severity as to alter a condition of employment by creating an "intimidating, hostile, or offensive working environment." The essence of a "hostile environment" claim is a "pattern or practice" of offensive behavior by the employer, a supervisor, co-workers, or non-employees so "severe or pervasive" as to interfere with the employee's job performance or create an abusive work environment.

In 1980, the federal agency responsible for enforcing Title VII issued guidelines prohibiting both *quid pro quo* and hostile environment sexual harassment.[7] The EEOC guidelines focus on sexuality rather than gender—in terms of job detriments resulting from "[u]nwelcome sexual advances, requests for sexual favors, and other verbal or physical behavior of a sexual nature"— and require that a "totality of the circumstances" be considered to determine whether particular conduct constitutes sexual harassment.[8] In addition, the EEOC anticipated judicial developments in hostile environment law when it eliminated tangible economic loss as a factor and provided that unwelcome sexual conduct violates Title VII whenever it "has the purpose or effect of unreasonably interfering with an individual's work performance or creating an intimidating, hostile, or offensive working environment." According to the EEOC guidelines, an employer is liable for both forms of sexual harassment when perpetrated by supervisors. The employer, however, is liable for harassment perpetrated by co-worker or nonemployees only if the employer knew or should have known of the harassment and failed to "take immediate and appropriate corrective action." They also recommend that employers take preventive measures to eliminate sexual harassment and state that employers may be liable to those denied employment opportunities or benefits given to another employee because of submission to sexual advances.[9]

In 1990, the EEOC issued policy guidance to elaborate on certain legal principles set forth in its interpretative guidelines from a decade before.[10] First, the later document reasserted the basic distinction between "quid pro quo" and "hostile environment" and states that an employer "will always be held responsible for acts of '*quid pro quo*' harassment by a supervisor while hostile environment cases require 'careful examination' of whether the harassing supervisor was acting in an 'agency capacity.'"[11] On the "welcomeness" issue, the policy guide states that "a contemporaneous complaint or protest" by the victim is an "important" but "not a necessary element of the claim." Instead, the Commission will look to all "objective evidence, rather than subjective, uncommunicated feelings" to "determine whether the victim's conduct is consistent, or inconsistent, with her assertion that the sexual conduct is unwelcome."[12] In determining whether a work environment is hostile, several factors are emphasized:

> (1) whether the conduct was verbal or physical or both; (2) how frequently it was repeated; (3) whether the conduct was hostile or patently offensive; (4) whether the alleged harasser was a co-worker or supervisor; (5) whether others joined in perpetrating the harassment; and (6) whether the harassment was directed at more than one individual.

However, because the alleged misconduct must "substantially interfere" with the victim's job performance, "sexual flirtation or innuendo, even vulgar language that is trivial or merely annoying, would probably not establish a hostile environment." In addition, "the harasser's conduct should be evaluated from the objective standard of a 'reasonable person.'"[13]

In 1999, the EEOC rescinded the employer liability rules of these earlier documents, in line with the *Faragher* and *Ellerth* decisions discussed below. The latest guidelines apply the same liability principles to all forms or illegal harassment—whether based on race, color, sex, religion, national origin, age, or disability—prohibited by federal anti-discrimination statutes.[14] In terms of substantive scope, the guidance emphasizes that harassment targeted against an individual because of sex need not involve sexual comments or conduct to be actionable. For example, the EEOC states that frequent, derogatory remarks about women may constitute unlawful harassment even if they are nonsexual in nature so long as they are sufficiently pervasive and are directed only at female (or male) employees because of their sex. Both the "supervisor" and "tangible employment action" necessary for imputing vicarious employer liability are broadly defined. Thus, the former includes any individual who has, or is regarded to have, the authority to affect an employee's work activities or status, whether directly or by recommendation to a final decision maker. The latter refers to any job detriment or benefit that results in significant change in employment status (e.g., a pay raise in exchange for sexual favors), but an unfulfilled threat by a supervisor is insufficient to be a "tangible employment action."

In addition, the employer has a duty of "reasonable care" to prevent and remedy harassment and, unless a very small employer, must establish, disseminate, and enforce a formal anti-harassment policy and complaint procedure, among other steps. Even an employer that promptly responds to a complaint has not taken reasonable care if it ignored prior complaints by other employees, or if it fails to screen supervisory applicants for any prior record of engaging in harassment. A harassment victim, on the other hand, must take advantage of any policy and procedures provided by the employer, and may be denied full monetary relief if she unreasonably delays in complaining. An employee may reasonably be excused from complaining, or for delay in doing so, only where there appears to be a risk of retaliation or other built-in obstacles making the complaint mechanism ineffective.

QUID PRO QUO HARASSMENT

The earliest judicial challenges involving tangible job detriment or *quid pro quo* harassment claims—filed by women who were allegedly fired for resisting sexual advances by their supervisors—were largely unsuccessful. The discriminatory conduct in such cases was deemed to arise from "personal proclivity" of the supervisor rather than "company directed policy which deprived women of employment opportunities." Until the mid-1970s, federal district courts were reluctant either to find a Title VII cause of action or to impose liability on employers who were neither in complicity with, nor had actual knowledge of, *quid pro quo* harassment by their supervisory employees. An historic turning point came when the federal district court in *Williams v. Saxbe* held for the first time that sexual harassment was discriminatory treatment within the meaning of Title VII because "it created an artificial barrier to employment which was placed before one gender and not the other, despite the fact that both genders were similarly situated."[15] Echoing earlier opinions that an employer is not liable for "interpersonal disputes between employees," the court nonetheless refused to dismiss the complaint since "if [the alleged harassment] was a policy or practice of plaintiff's supervisor, then it was the agency's policy or practice, which is prohibited by Title VII."[16]

Appellate tribunals in several federal circuits soon began to affirm that *quid pro quo* harassment violates Title VII where "gender is a substantial factor in the discrimination," reversing contrary lower court holdings. For example, in *Barnes v. Costle*, the D.C. Circuit disagreed with "the notion that employment conditions summoning sexual relations are somehow exempted from the coverage of Title VII."[17] Finding that it was "enough that gender is a factor contributing to the discrimination in a substantial way," the court ruled that differential treatment based upon an employee's rejection of her supervisor's sexual advances violated the statute. Similarly, in *Tomkins v. Public Service Electric & Gas Co.*, the Third Circuit reversed the trial court's denial of Title VII protection to all "sexual harassment and sexually motivated assault," finding that where an employee's "status as a female was a motivating factor in the supervisor's conditioning her continued employment on compliance with his sexual demands," actionable *quid pro quo* harassment had occurred.[18] "[T]o establish a *prima facie* case of *quid pro quo* harassment, a plaintiff must present evidence that she was subject to unwelcome sexual conduct, and that her reaction to that conduct was then used as the basis for decisions affecting the compensation, terms, conditions, or privileges of her employment."[19]

Where the conduct of the alleged harasser is motivated by factors other than the sex of the plaintiff, however, there may be no *quid pro quo* harassment. So-called "paramour" cases are a prime example. In *Piech v. Arthur Anderson & Co.*,[20] the court held that the plaintiff's inability to obtain a promotion, given instead to a female co-worker who was romantically involved with the employer, did not result from sex discrimination since all other employees, male or female, were equally affected. In contrast, the claim that females employed by the defendant had to extend sexual favors to succeed was cognizable as *quid pro quo* harassment. *Ellert v. University of Texas* similarly held that a secretary could not establish a *quid pro quo* harassment claim by alleging that her discharge resulted from her knowledge of the university dean's unwelcome advances towards an associate.[21] Even if the plaintiff's knowledge of the affair was the basis of action taken against her, it was not motivated by her gender and thus was not prohibited by Title VII.

While the loss of a "tangible employment benefit" has most often meant dismissal or demotion, *quid pro quo* claims may also arise from denial of career advantages—job title, duties, or assignments—of less immediate economic impact upon the employee. The Seventh Circuit, for example, has ruled that a tenured professor who was allegedly stripped of her job title and removed from academic committees because she rebuffed the sexual advances of the university provost may have a claim for *quid pro quo* sexual harassment under Title VII.[22] By contrast, the Fourth Circuit vacated a judgment in favor of the plaintiff in *Reingold v. Virginia*,[23] concluding that assigning her extra work, giving her inappropriate work assignments not included in her job description, and denying her the opportunity to attend a professional conference, did not amount to a "significant change in employment status." Generally speaking, the more remote or insubstantial the consequences of refusing a supervisor's unwelcome advances, the less likely that prerequisites for a *quid pro quo* will be found.[24]

The dismissal by Judge Susan Weber Wright of Paula Jones' sexual harassment lawsuit against former President Clinton squarely addressed the workplace consequences that must flow from the refusal to submit to an unwelcome sexual advance for the court to find actionable harassment.[25] Plaintiff Jones claimed that her career advancement had repeatedly been thwarted by her state employer as retribution for rebuffing the former Arkansas Governor.

As evidence of "tangible job detriments," Jones alleged that she had been discouraged by supervisors from seeking job promotions or pay increases; that following return from maternity leave, she was transferred to a new position with fewer responsibilities; that she was effectively denied access to grievance procedures available to other sexual harassment victims; and that by physically isolating her directly outside her supervisor's office with little work to do, she was "subjected to hostile treatment having tangible effects."

Judge Wright was unconvinced by the record, however, that any threat perceived by Jones during her alleged hotel meeting with the former Governor was so "clear and unambiguous" as to be a *quid pro quo* conditioning of "concrete job benefits or detriments on compliance with sexual demands." "Refusal" cases like *Jones*, calling for proof of "tangible job detriment" by plaintiffs who resist unwelcome sexual demands,[26] were distinguished from so-called "submission" cases, where "in the nature of things, economic harm will not be available to support the claim of the employee who submits to the supervisor's demands."[27]

It was widely anticipated that some further guidance on the essential character of *quid pro quo* harassment, particularly in relation to Jones' claims against President Clinton, would be forthcoming when the Supreme Court decided *Burlington Industries, Inc. v. Ellerth.*[28]

That case involved a former merchandising assistant at Burlington Industries who alleged that she was the subject of repeated boorish and offensive comments and gestures by a division vice-president who implied that her response to his advances would affect her career. Ellerth detailed three incidents in which her supervisor's comments could be construed as threats to deny her tangible job benefits.

A short time later, she quit her job without informing anyone in authority about the harassment, even though she was aware of Burlington's anti-harassment policy. Squarely presented by *Ellerth*, therefore, was the question of whether sexual advances by a supervisor accompanied by the threatened but not actualized loss of employment or job benefits may render an employer liable for *quid pro quo* harassment.

In fashioning an employer liability rule in *Ellerth*, the Court considered the judicial distinction between *quid pro quo* and environmental harassment to be less important than whether the claim involved a threat that had been "carried out" in fact.[29]

Such actions, according to the Court, include instances where the subordinate employee is subjected to "a significant change in employment status, such as hiring, firing, failing to promote, reassignment with significantly different responsibilities, or a decision causing a significant change in benefits" for failing to permit sexual liberties.[30]

Claims based on unfulfilled threats of retaliation were equated by the Court to hostile environment harassment, requiring plaintiff to prove "severe and pervasive" conduct.

Since Ellerth had not demonstrated that she was the victim of retaliation by her supervisor—in fact, she had been promoted during the period in question—there was no tangible detriment for which the employer could be held strictly liable.

The case was remanded, however, for application of an alternative standard of vicarious employer liability formulated by the Court for supervisory harassment cases not involving a "tangible employment action." Under that rule, after the plaintiff proves that the supervisory misconduct is both "severe and pervasive," the employer may assert as an "affirmative defense" that its actions to prevent and remedy workplace harassment were "reasonable," while the plaintiff "unreasonably" failed to take advantage of any anti-harassment policies and procedures of the employer.

Ellerth's failure to avail herself of the employer's grievance procedure likely defeated any Title VII recovery against Burlington under the second prong of this defense. The judicial task for lower courts after *Ellerth* is to construe this duty of reasonable care governing the employer's affirmative defense to liability. Other than rewarding employers for prophylactic measures aimed at workplace harassment and compelling victim participation in those efforts, *Ellerth* provides little specific guidance.

HOSTILE ENVIRONMENT HARASSMENT

The earlier judicial focus on economic detriment or *quid pro quo* harassment—making submission to sexual demands a condition to job benefits—largely gave way to Title VII claims for harassment that create an "intimidating, hostile, or offensive environment." The first federal appellate court to jettison the tangible economic loss requirement and recognize a hostile environment claim of sexual harassment was the D.C. Circuit in *Bundy v. Jackson.*[31] Despite the plaintiff's failure to prove *quid pro quo* harassment— she was not fired, demoted, or denied a promotion—the court refused to permit an employer to lawfully harass an employee "by carefully stopping short of firing the employee or taking any other tangible actions against her in response to her resistance."[32] Another decision important to the judicial development of sexually hostile environment law was *Henson v. Dundee*, in which the Eleventh Circuit rejected a claim of *quid pro quo* harassment but found that the employee had a right to a trial on the merits to determine whether the misconduct alleged made her job environment hostile.[33]

In *Meritor Savings Bank v. Vinson*,[34] the Supreme Court ratified the consensus then emerging among the federal circuits by recognizing a Title VII cause of action for sexual harassment. According to the Court, a "hostile environment," predicated on "purely psychological aspects of the workplace environment," could give rise to legal liability, and "tangible loss" of "an economic character" was not an essential element.[35] This holding was qualified by the Court with important reservations drawn from earlier administrative and judicial precedent. First, "not all workplace conduct that can be described as 'harassment' affects a term, condition, or privilege of employment within the meaning of Title VII." For example, the "mere utterance" of an "epithet" engendering "offensive feelings in an employee" would not ordinarily be *per se* actionable, the opinion suggests. Rather, the misconduct "must be sufficiently severe or pervasive to alter the conditions of [the victim's] employment and create an abusive working environment."[36]

Second, while "voluntariness" in the sense of consent is not a defense to a sexual harassment charge,

> [t]he gravamen of any sexual harassment claim is that the alleged sexual advances were 'unwelcome.' ... The correct inquiry is whether respondent by her conduct indicated that the alleged sexual advances

were unwelcome, not whether her actual participation in sexual intercourse was voluntary.[37]

Accordingly, "it does not follow that a complainant's sexually provocative speech or dress is irrelevant as a matter of law in determining whether he or she found particular sexual advances unwelcome. To the contrary, such evidence is obviously relevant."[38]

On the question of employer liability, the *Meritor Savings* majority held that the court below had "erred in concluding that employers are always automatically liable for sexual harassment by their supervisors."[39] The usual rule in Title VII cases is strict liability, and four Justices, concurring in the judgment, argued that the same rule should apply in the sexual harassment context as well. The majority disagreed, impliedly suggesting that in hostile environment cases no employer, at least none with a formal policy against harassment, should be made liable in the absence of actual or constructive knowledge.

The Supreme Court's failure to clearly define what constitutes a hostile environment in *Meritor Savings* led to frequent conflict in the lower courts, particularly as to the necessity of proving that serious psychological injury resulted from the harassing conduct.[40] The Court's decision in *Harris v. Forklift Systems, Inc.* revisited and offered some clarification of *Meritor Savings* in this regard.[41] In *Harris*, a company president had subjected a female manager to sexual innuendo, unwanted physical touching, and insults because of her gender. After two years, she left the job. In its decision, the Supreme Court decided that hostile environment sexual harassment need not "seriously affect psychological well-being" of the victim before Title VII is violated. According to the Court, *Meritor Savings* had adopted a "middle path" between condemning conduct that was "merely offensive" and requiring proof of "tangible psychological injury." Thus, a hostile environment is not created by the "mere utterance of an ... epithet which engenders offensive feelings in an employee." On the other hand, a victim of sexual harassment need not experience a "nervous breakdown" for the law to come into play. "So long as the environment would reasonably be perceived, and is perceived, as hostile or abusive, there is no need for it also to be psychologically injurious."[42]

Harris also addressed the standard of reasonableness to be applied in judging sexual harassment claims, another issue dividing the lower federal courts. The Court opted for a two-part analysis, both components of which must be met for a violation to be found. First, the conduct must create an objectively hostile work environment—"an environment that a reasonable person would find hostile and abusive." Second, the victim must subjectively perceive the environment to be abusive. The "totality of circumstances" surrounding the alleged harassment are to guide judicial inquiry, including "the frequency of the discriminatory conduct; its severity; whether it is physically threatening or humiliating or a mere offensive utterance; and whether it unreasonably interferes with an employee's work performance."[43]

Since *Meritor Savings* and *Harris*, a broad range of hostile environment harms—frequently as concerned with lewd comments, inquiries, jokes, or displays of pornographic materials in the workplace as with overt sexual aggression—have been brought before the federal courts. *Robinson v. Jackson Shipyards, Inc.*[44] was among the first reported decisions to impose liability for sexual harassment based on the pervasive presence of sexually oriented materials—magazine foldouts or other pictorial depictions—and "sexually demeaning remarks and jokes" by male coworkers without allegations of physical assaults or sexual propositions directed at the plaintiff. Most courts, however, have limited recovery to cases involving repeated sexual demands or other offensive conduct.[45] Except for cases involving touching or extreme verbal behavior, courts are often reluctant to find that sexual derision—or claims against pornography in the workplace—is sufficient to create a hostile environment when unaccompanied by sexual demands.[46] The First Amendment has even been invoked to curb harassment claims founded solely on verbal insults or pictorial or literary matter, as impermissible content-based restrictions on free speech.[47] This tendency may be reinforced by the Court's admonition in *Oncale v. Sundowner Offshore Services* that Congress never intended Title VII to become a general "code of civility." Conduct need not be overtly sexual, however, as other hostile conduct directed against the victim because of the victim's sex is also prohibited.[48] And, in line with *Meritor Savings*, evidence of a sexual harassment claimant's own provocative behavior or prior workplace conduct is generally relevant to a judicial determination of whether the defendant's conduct was unwelcome.[49]

Likewise, claims involving isolated or intermittent incidents have frequently been dismissed as insufficiently pervasive. A recurring point in the decisions is that "simple teasing, offhand comments, and isolated incidents (unless extremely serious) will not amount to discriminatory changes in the 'terms and conditions of employment.'"[50] In *Jones v. Clinton*, for example, the court ruled that considering the "totality of the circumstances," an alleged hotel incident and other encounters between Paula Jones and former President (then-Governor) Clinton were not "the kind of sustained and nontrivial conduct necessary for a claim of hostile work environment."[51] In particular, the court noted that plaintiff Jones "never missed a day of work" because of the incident nor did she complain to her supervisors; never did she seek medical or psychological treatment as a consequence of alleged harassment; and that her allegations generally failed to demonstrate any adverse workplace effects. The Seventh Circuit, in another case, concluded that while an Illinois state employee "subjectively perceived her work environment to be hostile and abusive" the paucity of sexually oriented comments complained of—three suggestive comments by a co-worker over a three-month period—"were not sufficiently severe that a reasonable person would feel subjected to a hostile working environment."[52] Of course, a single incident may be actionable if it is linked to a granting or denial of an employment benefit (*quid pro quo* harassment), or if the incident involves physical assault or other exceptional circumstances.[53] The EEOC policy statement also states that the agency "will presume that the unwelcome, intentional touching of a charging party's intimate body areas is sufficiently offensive to alter the conditions of her working environment and constitute a violation of Title VII."[54]

SAME-SEX HARASSMENT

Title VII was interpreted early on by the courts and the EEOC to protect both men and women against workplace sexual harassment by the opposite sex. In *Meritor Savings,* the Court found that Congress intended "to strike at the entire spectrum of disparate treatment of men and women" in employment and read Title VII to prohibit discriminatory harassment by a supervisor "because of the subordinate's sex." Until the Supreme Court decision in *Oncale v. Sundowner Offshore Services, Inc.,* however, federal courts were sharply divided over whether the act applied when the harasser and the victim are of the same sex. Although Title VII does not prohibit direct discrimination by an employer based on an employee's sexual orientation[55]—whether homosexual, bisexual, or heterosexual—several federal appellate and trial courts found that same-sex harassment was actionable in some circumstances. In effect, "because of" sex in Title VII reached all disparate treatment based on the sex or gender of the employee, without regard to whether the harasser is male or female.[56] The Fifth Circuit, on the other hand, concluded that same-sex harassment could never form the basis of a Title VII claim.[57]

In *Oncale v. Sundowner Offshore Services, Inc.*, the U.S. Supreme Court agreed with the majority view of the federal courts that "nothing in Title VII necessarily bars a claim of discrimination 'because of ... sex' merely because the plaintiff and the defendant (or the person charged with acting on behalf of the defendant) are of the same sex."[58] The case involved *quid pro quo* and hostile environment claims of a male offshore oil rig worker who alleged that he was sexually assaulted and abused by his supervisor and two male co-workers, forcing him to quit his job. Although the Court acknowledged that Congress was "assuredly" not concerned with male-onmale sexual harassment when it enacted Title VII, it found no justification in the statutory language or the Court's precedents for excluding same-sex harassment claims from the coverage of Title VII. The opinion for the Court is notable for its emphasis on general sexual harassment principles, possibly paving the way for stricter scrutiny of sexual harassment claims in general. First, the opinion observes that federal discrimination laws do not prohibit "all verbal or physical harassment in the workplace," only conduct that is discriminatory and based on sex. Moreover, harassing or offensive conduct "is not automatically discrimination because of sex, merely because the words used have a sexual content or connotation." Instead, the Court emphasized, those alleging harassment must prove that the conduct was not just offensive, but "actually constituted" discrimination.[59] Second, reiterating *Meritor Savings* and *Harris*, only conduct so "severe or pervasive" and objectively offensive as to alter the conditions of the victim's employment is actionable so that "courts and juries do not mistake ordinary socializing in the workplace—such as male-on-male horseplay or intersexual flirtation—for discriminatory `conditions of employment.'"[60] Another moderating aspect of the *Oncale* ruling is the Court's obvious concern for "social context" and workplace realities when appraising all sexual harassment claims—same-sex or otherwise.[61]

The full implications of *Oncale* for same sex harassment and hostile environment cases remain largely unsettled. The Court clearly reinjected the element of discrimination—"because of sex"— back into harassment law, perhaps tempering a tendency on the part of some lower courts to equate offensive behavior with a hostile environment without more. Indeed, the opinion states that "Title VII does not prohibit all verbal or physical harassment" and "requires neither asexuality or androgyny in the workplace." Because little guidance was offered, however, for determining when untoward conduct crosses the line to sex-based discrimination, lower courts have been left to grapple with the issue. The Court's opinion suggests two possible approaches to demonstrating a nexus between sexually offensive conduct and gender discrimination.

A trier of fact might reasonably find such discrimination, for
example, if a female victim is harassed in such sex-specific and
derogatory terms by another woman as to make it clear that the harasser
is motivated by general hostility to the presence of women in the
workplace. A same-sex harassment plaintiff may also, of course, offer
direct comparative evidence about how the alleged harasser treated
members of both sexes in a mixed-sex workplace.

It is difficult, however, to discern how either approach would aid male
same-sex plaintiffs like *Oncale* in proving discrimination "because of sex"
when they are victims of harassment by other males on an oil rig or in other
male-dominated workplaces.

The *Oncale* ruling also marked a general tempering of earlier decisions
driving current trends in sexual harassment litigation. The numerous examples
cited by the Court of "innocuous differences" in the way men and women
interact might serve as the basis for future judicial acceptance of a wider
latitude of behavior in the workplace than might otherwise have been
considered permissible. The lengths to which the opinion seems to go in
articulating the bounds of permissible heterosexual behavior in a same-sex
harassment case reinforces this conclusion. Thus, the express approval of
"intersexual flirtation" and "teasing or roughhousing" implies that a certain
level of fraternization in the workplace is permissible and the consequent
range of actionable conduct correspondingly reduced. In this regard, the
decision's emphasis upon "social context" may complicate the already
difficult judicial task of identifying a sexually hostile work environment. Does
this mean, for example, that conduct permitted in a blue-collar workplace may
be actionable in a white-collar, professional environment? Thus, the decision
might lead to the dismissal of cases the courts have entertained in the past. At
the very least, beyond its threshold endorsement of a same-sex cause of action
under Title VII, the *Oncale* decision appears to raise as many questions as it
answers.

Lower courts have offered answers to some of those questions. As *Oncale*
emphasizes, the object of Title VII is elimination of discrimination "because of
sex." Thus, inappropriate conduct that targets both sexes, or is inflicted
regardless of sex, is not covered. The statute does not reach the "equal
opportunity" or "bisexual" harasser who treats male and female employees the
same, however inappropriately.[62] Harassment is "because of" sex only if the
gender of the victim is the motivating or "but for" cause of the offensive
conduct.[63] That offensive workplace conduct may be more offensive—or have
a disparate impact—on female than male employees may not suffice if an

intention to discriminate is lacking.[64] For example, in *Kestner v. Stanton Group, Inc.,*[65] a female employee complained about a male manager's abusive demeanor and constant yelling. Although the manager had also made several sexually suggestive and crude remarks that were gender-specific, the Sixth Circuit concluded: "That [the manager] yelled at employees, male and female, and that he cursed in front of employees, male and female, does not by itself create a hostile work environment."[66]

Similarly, the courts have generally reiterated the position that Title VII provides no remedy to a person claiming harassment at the hands of co-workers motivated solely by hostility to his perceived sexual orientation.[67] "Gender" is not to be equated with "sexual orientation" under Title VII. In *Spearman v. Ford Motor Co.,*[68] the plaintiff claimed that he had been subjected to vulgar and sexually explicit insults and graffiti by his co-workers who, he alleged, perceived him to be too feminine to fit the male image in a manufacturing plant. But because the employee's problems were found to stem from an altercation over work issues and because of his apparent homosexuality, rather than sex, the Seventh Circuit dismissed the action. If the plaintiff can show that the harassment was based on his or her failure to conform to gender stereotypes, however, an action for sexual harassment may be allowed.

The Supreme Court has denounced sexual stereotyping under Title VII in a failure to promote case,[69] and several federal appellate courts have applied the same rationale in the harassment setting. In *Nichols v. Azteca Restaurant Enterprizes, Inc.,*[70] a male restaurant employee was addressed by his coworkers as a female and was taunted for his feminine manner of walk and serving customers, in addition to being subjected to derogatory comments based on his sexual orientation. The court ultimately found that the harassment at issue was closely linked to gender because the plaintiff's harassers discriminated against him for being too feminine.

In a subsequent case, however, the Ninth Circuit *en banc* largely disregarded sexual stereotypes, focusing instead on the "unwelcome physical conduct of a sexual nature" to permit a gay man to pursue an harassment claim. The plaintiff in *Rene v. MGM Grand Hotel*[71] was a former butler who claimed his supervisor and several fellow employees on an all male staff engaged in offensive gestures and touched his body "like they would to a woman."

In this "sexual touching hostile environment" case, the appellate court ruled, the sexual orientation of the victim was "irrelevant," since "[t]he physical attacks to which Rene was subjected, which targeted body parts clearly linked to his sexuality, were 'because of ... sex.'"[72] Three judges concurred in the result, but wrote separately that the employee could sue for gender-stereotyping harassment as in *Nichols*. In both cases, they stated, a male employee was mocked for his mannerisms and addressed by coworkers in female terms "to remind [him] that he did not conform to their gender-based stereotypes."[73]

Instead of animosity or ridicule, post-*Oncale* courts have also considered issues raised by employees who are subjected to unwelcome displays of affection or sexual advances by supervisors or coworkers of the same sex. This has likewise required a judicial determination as to the motivation behind the alleged discriminatory conduct—whether based on gender or sex, which is prohibited by Title VII, or sexual orientation, which is not. In *Oncale,* the Supreme Court noted that one way by which a plaintiff can prove that an incident of same-sex harassment constitutes sex discrimination is to show that the alleged harasser made explicit or implicit proposals of sexual activity and provide "credible evidence" that the harasser was homosexual.

In *Shepherd v. Slater Steels Corp.*,[74] the Seventh Circuit permitted the case to go to trial on evidence that the harasser's action was based on sexual attraction, such as repeated remarks that the plaintiff was a "handsome young man," coupled with other encounters of a sexual nature. The Fifth Circuit has decided that there are two types of evidence that are likely to be "especially [credible] proof" that the harasser may be a homosexual.[75]

The first type is evidence suggesting that the harasser intended to have some kind of sexual contact with the plaintiff, rather than "merely to humiliate him for reasons unrelated to sexual interest." Second is proof that the alleged harasser made same-sex advances to others, particularly other employees. According to the court, a harasser might make sexually demeaning remarks and putdowns for sex-neutral reasons, but it is less likely that sexual advances would be made without regard to sex.

Other courts have required the plaintiff to demonstrate that the harassment was motivated by sexual desire.[76] Suffice it to say, considerable confusion persists among the lower courts as to whether gender, sexual attraction, or conduct of a sexual nature is the key factor distinguishing discrimination based on sex from sexual orientation discrimination in the same-sex harassment context.

To a large extent, the answer may depend on the facts presented by the particular case.

REMEDIES

In 1991, Congress enacted amendments to the Civil Rights Act of 1964.[77] Of particular importance to sexual harassment claimants, the amendments established jury trials and compensatory and punitive damages as remedies for Title VII violations. Previously, Title VII plaintiffs had no right to a jury trial and were entitled only to equitable relief in the form of injunctions against future employer misconduct, reinstatement, and limited backpay for any loss of income resulting from any discharge, denial of promotion, or other adverse employment decision. Consequently, victims of alleged sexual harassment were often compelled to rely on state fair employment practices laws,[78] or traditional common law causes of action for assault, intentional infliction of emotional distress, unlawful interference with contract, invasion of privacy, and the like, to obtain complete monetary relief.[79] Section 102 of the 1991 amendments altered the focus of federal EEO enforcement from reliance on judicial injunctions, where voluntary conciliation efforts fail, to jury trials, and compensatory and punitive damages in Title VII actions involving intentional discrimination.[80]

Compensatory damages under the 1991 Act include "future pecuniary losses, emotional pain, suffering, inconvenience, mental anguish, loss of enjoyment of life, and other nonpecuniary losses."[81] The compensatory and punitive damages provided by §102 are "in addition to any relief authorized by Section 706(g)" of the 1964 Civil Rights Act.[82] The 1991 amendments further state that "[c]ompensatory damages awarded under [§1981a] shall not include backpay, interest on backpay, or any other type of relief authorized under section 706(g)." Therefore, plaintiffs may recover damages in addition to equitable relief, including backpay. Punitive damages may also be recovered against private employers where the plaintiff can demonstrate that the employer acted "with malice or reckless indifference" to the individual's federally protected rights. Punitive damages are not recoverable, however, against a governmental entity.[83] In cases where a plaintiff seeks compensatory or punitive damages, any party may demand a jury trial.[84]

The damages remedy under the law is limited by dollar amount, however, according to the size of the defendant employer during the 20 or more calendar weeks in the current or preceding calendar year. The sum of compensatory and punitive damages awarded may not exceed: $50,000 in the case of an employer with more than 14 and fewer than 101 employees; $100,000 in the case of an employer with more than 100 and fewer than 201 employees; $200,000 in the case of an employer with more than 200 and fewer than 501 employees; and $300,000 in the case of an employer with more than 500 employees.[85] In jury trial cases, the court may not inform the jury of the damage caps set forth in the statute.

In *Pollard v. E.I. duPont de Nemours & Co.,*[86] the Supreme Court significantly expanded the amount of monetary relief that may be awarded victims of sexual harassment or other forms of intentional discrimination prohibited by Title VII. Prior to that decision, there was a dispute among the circuits as to whether "front pay" in lieu of reinstatement was authorized by §706(g) of Title VII, or was included in "compensatory damages" and subject to the $300,000 cap imposed by the 1991 Act.[87] Front pay is money awarded for lost compensation during the period between judgment for a Title VII plaintiff and the plaintiff's reinstatement, or money awarded when reinstatement is impractical. When reinstatement is not immediately available, front pay is paid until the plaintiff is reinstated. In some instances, however, reinstatement may not be a viable option at all. Continuing hostility between the plaintiff and the employer or co-workers, or psychological injuries suffered as a result of discrimination, may prevent the plaintiff's return to the workplace. Front pay in such circumstances is a substitute for reinstatement.

The plaintiff in *Pollard* had claimed that she was a victim of co-worker harassment and that her supervisors were aware of the illegal conduct. As a consequence, she was given a medical leave of absence for psychological assistance but was later fired for refusing to return to what she claimed was a hostile work environment. At trial, Pollard was awarded $300,000 in compensatory damages—the maximum allowable—for emotional and psychological suffering but was denied any additional front pay because of the cap. The Sixth Circuit affirmed the result.

In a unanimous decision, the Supreme Court concluded that front pay is not an element of compensatory damages within the meaning of the 1991 Act, thus ruling that the statutory cap did not apply. Tracing the history of Title VII, the Court noted that the original statute authorized backpay awards, which had been interpreted by the courts to include front pay to a date certain in the future as an alternative to reinstatement. To limit front pay to cases where there is eventual reinstatement after judgment, reasoned the Court, would leave the most egregious offenders subject to the least sanctions. Likewise, a ruling that front pay could be considered compensation for "future pecuniary losses" subject to the damages cap would fly in the face of the congressional intent behind the 1991 Act "to expand the available remedies by permitting the recovery of compensatory and punitive damages in addition to previously available remedies, such as front pay." The consequences of *Pollard* for employers may be considerable. The estimated monetary value of harassment or other intentional discrimination cases may be multiplied several times if juries or judges can be persuaded by plaintiffs' attorneys to award front pay for years, or even decades, into the future.[88]

The expansion of Title VII remedies dramatically affects the level of relief available in cases of intentional sex discrimination, where for the first time employees in the private sector have the prospect of federal compensatory and punitive damage recoveries and the right to a jury trial. The act now provides a monetary remedy for victims of sexual harassment in employment in addition to lost wages. Since harassment of the hostile environment type often occurs without economic loss to the employee, in terms of pay or otherwise, critics of the prior law charged that the sexual harassment victim was frequently without any effective federal relief. Title VII plaintiffs may now seek monetary compensation for emotional pain and suffering, and other pecuniary and nonpecuniary losses, caused by sexual harassment. Moreover, federal claims may be joined with pendent state-law claims for damages unlimited by the caps in the federal law or an election made between pursuing state and federal remedies.

LIABILITY OF EMPLOYERS AND SUPERVISORS FOR MONETARY DAMAGES

The addition of monetary damages to the arsenal of Title VII remedies rekindled inquiry into an employer's liability for harassment perpetrated by its supervisors and nonsupervisory employees and the personal liability of individual harassers. The *Ellerth* decision ratified the federal circuit courts, which had generally declared employers vicariously liable for *quid pro quo* sexual harassment committed by supervisors culminating in tangible job detriment.[89] Only those with actual authority to hire, promote, discharge, or affect the terms and conditions of employment can engage in *quid pro quo* harassment and are held to act as agents of the employer, regardless of their motivations. *Quid pro quo* harassment is viewed no differently than other forms of prohibited discrimination for which employers have routinely been held vicariously liable. Because Title VII defines employer to include "any agent" of the employer, the statute is understood to have incorporated the principle of *respondeat superior*, in effect holding "employers liable for the discriminatory [acts of] ... supervisory employees whether or not the employer knew, should have known, or approved of the supervisor's actions."[90] However, the suggestion in *Meritor Savings* that courts look to agency law in developing liability rules for hostile work environment led most lower federal courts to reject vicarious liability for employers lacking actual or constructive knowledge of environmental harassment perpetrated by a supervisor. Prior to *Ellerth* and *Faragher*, most courts made an employer liable for a hostile environment only if it knew or should have known about the harassment and failed to take prompt remedial action to end it.

Vicarious Employer Liability: the *Ellerth/Faragher* Affirmative Defense

A different set of liability principles was adopted by the Supreme Court for supervisory harassment in *Ellerth* (discussed above) and *Faragher v. City of Boca Raton*.[91] While working for the City of Boca Raton, Faragher and her female colleagues were subjected to offensive touching, comments, and gestures from two supervisors. Although Faragher did not complain to department management at the time of her employment, when she resigned from her position for reasons unrelated to the alleged harassment, Faragher sued the city under Title VII.

As in *Ellerth*, the *Faragher* Court largely abandoned the legal distinction between *quid pro quo* and hostile environment harassment, looking instead to agency principles as guides to employer liability for supervisory misconduct. The Court reiterated *Ellerth's* determination that sexual harassment by a supervisor is not within the scope of employment. But because a supervisor is "aided" in his actions by the agency relationship, a more stringent vicarious liability standard was warranted than pertains to similar misconduct by mere co-workers, where the employer is liable for negligence only if he fails to abate conditions of which he "knew or should have known." "When a person with supervisory authority discriminates in the terms and conditions of subordinates' employment, his actions necessarily draw upon his superior position over the people who report to him, or those under them, whereas an employee generally cannot check a supervisor's abusive conduct the same way that she might deal with abuse from a co-worker."[92]

The Court also determined, however, that public policy considerations were important in crafting employer liability rules. The congressional design behind Title VII favored both the creation of anti-harassment policies and effective grievance mechanisms by employers, and a coordinate duty on the part of employees to avoid or mitigate harm. To accommodate these Title VII policies and agency principles of employers' vicarious liability, the Court in *Ellerth* and *Faragher* adopted a composite standard which for the first time explicitly allows employers an affirmative defense to liability for environmental harassment caused by supervisory misconduct. According to the Court:

> An employer is subject to vicarious liability to a victimized employee for an actionable hostile environment created by a supervisor with immediate (or successively higher) authority over the employee. When no tangible employment action is taken, a defending employer may raise an affirmative defense to liability or damages, subject to proof by a preponderance of the evidence.... The defense comprises two necessary elements: (a) that the employer exercised reasonable care to prevent and correct promptly any sexually harassing behavior, and (b) that the plaintiff employee unreasonably failed to take advantage of any preventative or corrective opportunities provided by the employer or to avoid harm otherwise. While proof that an employer had promulgated an antiharassment policy with complaint procedure is not necessary in every instance as a matter of law, the need for a stated policy suitable to the employment circumstances may appropriately be addressed in any case when litigating the first element of the defense. And while proof that an employee failed to fulfill the corresponding obligation of reasonable care to avoid harm is not limited to showing an unreasonable failure to use any complaint procedure provided by the employer, a demonstration of such failure will normally suffice to satisfy the employer's burden under the second element of the defense.[93]

The affirmative defense is unavailable, however, and employers are strictly liable for harassment of subordinate employees by their supervisors perpetrated by means of a "tangible employment action," such as discharge, demotion, or undesirable reassignment.

The affirmative defense adopted by the Court in *Ellerth* and *Faragher* imposes a duty of care on both the employer and the employees to prevent workplace harassment and to mitigate its effects. The first line of defense for the employer is to adopt and communicate to its staff and management an effective sexual harassment policy and complaint procedure. In most cases, the failure to do so—at least in the case of large employers, like the city government in *Faragher*— will result in strict liability for any harassing conduct by supervisory employees, whether or not the alleged victim suffers any adverse employment action. Questions remain, however, as to the scope of that legal obligation, particularly in relation to smaller employers, since the

Court's formulation appears to leave open the possibility that corrective actions short of a formalized anti-harassment policy may be reasonable, at least in some circumstances. Thus, considerations of employer size and resources, and the structure of the workplace (e.g., whether a single location or on scattered sites) may be relevant factors.

Similarly, the latest High Court decisions place the burden on aggrieved employees to avail themselves of corrective procedures provided by the employer—thereby mitigating damages caused by the alleged harassment—or risk having their claim legally barred. However, the Court did not address whether an employee's failure to take such saving action would be deemed "unreasonable" if the complainant is able to demonstrate the inadequacy of the employer's grievance procedure, if employees had suffered retaliation for invoking the procedure in the past, or if harassing supervisors previously had not been disciplined for their action. Nor do the decisions specifically address the fate of employers denied the benefit of the affirmative defense because an employee followed the complaint procedure set forth in the employer's anti-harassment policy. Is strict employer liability the rule in such cases, or is the issue to be decided in light of the overall appropriateness of the employer's remedial response? Thus, many questions remain for lower courts to decide in regard to the employer's assertion of an affirmative defense. Consequently, while clarifying the law to some extent, it may take the courts years to flesh out the concept of "reasonable care," "correct promptly," "unreasonably failed," and "tangible employment action," all key elements in the Court's definition of the employer's affirmative defense.

Some guidance may be gleaned from later federal appeals court decisions that have grappled with issues left unresolved by *Ellerth* and *Faragher*. Much judicial attention has focused on whether conduct alleged by the plaintiff amounts to a tangible employment action, nullifying the employer's affirmative defense, and to the adequacy of any corrective action taken by the employer in response to alleged harassment. Aside from hiring, discharge, promotion or demotion, and benefits decisions having direct economic consequences, an employment action may be "tangible" if it results in a significant change in employment status.[94]

In addition, most courts have read *Ellerth* to require, at a minimum, that the employer establish, disseminate, and enforce an anti-harassment policy and complaint procedure.[95] Beyond adopting an anti-harassment policy and procedures for its employees, the employer must undertake immediate and appropriate corrective action—including discipline proportionate to the seriousness of the offense—when it learns of a violation.[96] Whether the employer has responded in a prompt and reasonable manner depends on all the underlying facts and circumstances, and the harassment victim's own conduct may be a relevant factor.[97] In some cases, alleged harassers who were discharged but later exonerated have sued their employers. The employer has usually prevailed, however, as long as the decision to fire or otherwise discipline the suspected perpetrator was based on a good faith belief of misconduct after an adequate investigation was performed.[98] Even before the High Court's latest decisions, lower court rulings suggested that the most effective defensive strategy for employers to avoid liability for a hostile work environment was a proactive approach.[99] In addition, the courts have generally been reluctant to impose Title VII liability on employers who act "prophylactically" to stem harassing conditions before they begin.[100]

The practical lesson for employers is to formulate and communicate to employees a specific policy forbidding workplace harassment; to establish procedures for reporting incidents of harassment that bypass the immediate supervisor of the victim if he or she is the alleged harasser; to immediately investigate all alleged incidents and order prompt corrective action (including make-whole relief for the victim) when warranted; and to appropriately discipline the harasser.

Finally, the Court continued to build on its holdings in *Faragher* and *Ellerth* in *Kolstad v. American Dental Association.*[101] Addressing the availability of punitive damages for violations of Title VII, the Court concluded that although an employer may be vicariously liable for the misconduct of its supervisory employees, it will not be subject to punitive damages if it has made good faith efforts to comply with Title VII. The Court noted that subjecting employers that adopt antidiscrimination policies to punitive damages would undermine Title VII's objective of encouraging employers to prevent discrimination in the workplace.

Constructive Discharge

In 2004, the Supreme Court resolved a conflict among the federal circuits concerning the defenses, if any, that may be available to an employer against an employee's claim that she was forced to resign because of "intolerable" sexual harassment at the hands of a supervisor. In *Pennsylvania State Police v. Suders,*[102] the plaintiff claimed that the tangible adverse action was supervisory harassment so severe that it drove the employee to quit, a constructive discharge in effect. The Court accepted the theory of a constructive discharge as a tangible employment action, but it also set conditions under which the employer could assert an affirmative defense and avoid strict liability under Title VII. The issue is of key importance for determining the scope of employers' vicarious liability in "supervisory" sexual harassment cases alleging a hostile work environment.

As noted, *Farager* and *Ellerth* held employers strictly liable for a sexually hostile work environment created by a supervisor, when the challenged discrimination or harassment results in a "tangible employment action." The Court defined that term categorically to mean any "significant change in employment status" that may—but not always—result in economic harm. Specifically, included were "hiring, firing, failing to promote, reassignment with significantly different responsibilities, or a decision causing a significant change in benefits."[103] However, a "constructive discharge," where the employee quits, claiming that conditions are so intolerable that he or she was effectively "fired," presented an unresolved issue. Could an employer, faced with a claim of constructive discharge, still assert the *Ellerth/Farager* defense?

The constructive discharge doctrine originated in federal labor law and was later transposed by judicial interpretation to employment discrimination cases. Basically, the courts have held that an employee alleging a constructive discharge must demonstrate the concurrence of two factors: (1) the employee suffered harassment or discrimination so intolerable that a reasonable person in the same position would have felt compelled to resign and (2) the employee's reaction to the workplace situation was reasonable given the totality of circumstances. Because of its direct economic harm on employees, the Third Circuit in *Suders* joined the Eighth Circuit,[104] concluding that constructive discharge, if proven, is the functional equivalent of an actual dismissal and amounts to a tangible employment action. Taking the opposite position, the Second and Sixth Circuits had decided that a voluntary resignation, as opposed to a dismissal, was never the kind of official action that deprived the employer of its legal defenses.[105] The opposing circuits refused to view constructive discharge as a tangible employment action because it is a "unilateral" act of the employee that is neither instigated nor ratified by the employer.

In *Suders*, the Court applied the framework of its 1998 rulings to stake out a middle ground between the conflicting approaches to constructive discharge taken by the courts of appeals. The only real difference between the harassment in *Ellerth/Farager* and this case was one of degree; that is, *Suders* presented a "worst case" scenario, or harassment "racheted up to the breaking point." But a constructive discharge claim requires more than a pattern of severe or pervasive workplace abuse as would satisfy the legal standard for ordinary harassment. Employees advancing "compound" claims must also prove that the abusive working environment became so intolerable that a reasonable person would have felt compelled to resign. Such objectively intolerable conditions could result from co-worker conduct, unofficial supervisory act, or "official" company acts. The Court's earlier decisions applied agency principles to define employer vicarious liability for a supervisor's harassment of subordinates. Only when supervisory misconduct is "aided by the agency relation," as evidenced by a tangible or "official act of the enterprise," is the employer's responsibility so obvious as to warrant strict liability. When no tangible employment action is taken, the basis for imputing blame on the employer is less evident, and the focus shifts to the Title VII policy of prevention. The employer may then defeat vicarious liability by showing that it had reasonable anti-harassment procedures in place that the employee unreasonably failed to utilize.

Ultimately, the Court held that Title VII encompasses employer liability for constructive discharge claims attributable to a supervisor, but ruled that an "employer does not have recourse to the *Ellerth/Faragher* affirmative defense when a supervisor's official act precipitates the constructive discharge; absent such a 'tangible employment action,' however, the defense is available to the employer whose supervisors are charged with harassment."[106] In recognizing hostile environment constructive discharge claims, *Suders* enhanced Title VII protection for employees who quit their jobs over intense sexual harassment by a supervisor. But the decision also makes it easier for an employer to defend against such claims by showing that it has reasonable procedures for reporting and correcting harassment of which the employee failed to avail herself. Only "if the plaintiff quits in reasonable response to an employer-sanctioned adverse action officially changing her employment status or situation, for example, a humiliating demotion, extreme cut in pay, or transfer to a position in which she would face unbearable working condition," is the employer made strictly liable for monetary damages or other Title VII relief.[107]

Moreover, even where there has been a tangible employment action, coupled with a constructive discharge or resignation, the employer may have defenses available. First, the employer may argue that the harassing conduct did not occur as alleged, or was not sufficiently severe, pervasive, or unwelcome to meet standards for a Title VII violation. Second, if the tangible employment action is shown to be unrelated to the alleged harassment, or is taken for legitimate non-discriminatory reasons—particularly, if by persons other than the alleged harasser—the employer might escape liability. Finally, the employer might be able to demonstrate that, whatever form the underlying supervisory harassment may take, it did not meet the standard for constructive discharge: "so intolerable that a reasonable person would have felt compelled to resign." But *Suders* also makes it more difficult to obtain summary judgment and avoid jury trials in sexual harassment cases involving constructive discharge claims. Under the decision, if there is any real dispute about whether the employee suffered a tangible employment action, the employer may not rely on the affirmative defense to obtain summary judgment.

Personal Liability of Harassing Supervisors and Co-workers

Because the term "agent" is included within the definition of "employer," some division of judicial opinion initially existed regarding the personal liability of individual supervisors and coworkers for hostile environment harassment or other discriminatory conduct. However, all of the federal circuit courts to address the question eventually interpreted the term "agent" in the statutory definition as merely incorporating *respondeat superior* and refused to impose personal liability on agents.[108] These courts also note the incongruity of imposing personal liability on individuals while capping compensatory and punitive damages based on employer size, as the statute does, and exempting small businesses that employ less than 15 persons from Title VII altogether.

RETALIATION

Under Title VII, it is unlawful for employers to discriminate or retaliate against an employee "because he has opposed any practice made an unlawful employment practice [under Title VII] ... or because he has made a charge, testified, assisted, or participated in any manner in an investigation, proceeding, or hearing under [Title VII]."[109] The scope of this retaliation provision was the subject of judicial debate for a number of years. In 2006, however, the Supreme Court issued its decision in *Burlington Northern and Santa Fe Railway Co. v. White*,[110] a case that involved a plaintiff who alleged that her employer had unlawfully retaliated against her by reassigning her to a less desirable position after she had made several complaints about sexual harassment on the job.

In a 9-0 decision with one justice concurring, the Court held that the statute's retaliation provision encompasses any employer action that "would have been materially adverse to a reasonable employee or job applicant."[111] This standard, which is much broader than a standard that would have confined the retaliation provision to actions that affect only the terms and conditions of employment, generally makes it easier to sue employers if they retaliate against workers who complain about discrimination. Under the Court's interpretation, employees must establish only that the employer's actions might dissuade a worker from making a charge of discrimination. This means that an employee may successfully sue an employer for retaliation even if the employer's action does not actually result in an adverse employment action, such as being fired or losing wages.

In 2008, the Court issued a decision in *Crawford v. Metropolitan Government of Nashville and Davidson County*,[112] a case in which the plaintiff alleged that her participation in a sexual harassment investigation against her supervisor resulted in her termination. Although the plaintiff cooperated in the investigation and provided testimony regarding explicit comments and actions made by her boss, the fact that she had not filed the sexual harassment complaint or other charges with the Equal Employment Opportunity Commission (EEOC) led the lower court to rule that she was not covered under Title VII's retaliation provision. In reversing the decision, the Court held that Title VII's retaliation provision encompasses retaliation against "an employee who speaks out about discrimination not on her own initiative, but in answering questions during an employer's internal investigation."[113] The Court emphasized that this result would prevent employers from undermining the purpose of Title VII by silencing employees who might fear being penalized if they reported discrimination during the course of an investigation.[114]

SEXUAL HARASSMENT IN THE SCHOOLS

Title IX of the 1972 Education Amendments provides that "[no] person in the United States shall, on the basis of sex, be excluded from participation in, be denied the benefits of, or be subjected to discrimination under any education program or activity receiving Federal financial assistance,"[115] and the statute has been interpreted to provide a basis for challenging sexual harassment in classrooms and on campuses. The Court's recent decisions involving Title IX address various issues, including employer liability and the availability of damages and other statutory remedies.

Under Title IX, student victims of any form of sex discrimination, including sexual harassment, may file a written complaint with the Office of Civil Rights (OCR) for administrative determination and possible imposition of sanctions—including termination of federal funding— upon the offending educational institution.[116] In addition, school personnel who harass students may be sued individually for monetary damages and other civil remedies under 42 U.S.C. §1983, which prohibits the deprivation of federally protected rights under "color of law."

In addition to making administrative sanctions available, Title IX provides student victims with an avenue of judicial relief. In *Cannon v. University of Chicago*,[117] the Supreme Court ruled that an implied right of action exists under Title IX for student victims of sex discrimination who need not exhaust their administrative remedies before filing suit.[118] However, the availability of monetary damages under Title IX remained uncertain until *Franklin v. Gwinnett County Public Schools*.[119] In *Franklin*, a female high school student brought an action for damages under Title IX against her school district alleging that she had been subjected to sexual harassment and abuse by a teacher. Although the harassment became known and an investigation was conducted, teachers and administrators did not act and the petitioner was subsequently discouraged from pressing charges. The Court, which found that sexual harassment by a teacher constituted discrimination on the basis of sex, held that damages were available to the sexual harassment victim if she could prove that the school district had intentionally violated Title IX.

After *Franklin*, it was clear that sexual harassment by a teacher constituted sex discrimination, but the extent to which school districts could be held liable for misconduct by its employees was less clear. The appropriate standard for measuring a school district's liability for sexual abuse of a student by a teacher remained unsettled until the Supreme Court ruling in *Gebser v. Lago Vista Independent School District*.[120] In *Gebser,* the Supreme Court answered the question of what standard of liability to apply to school districts under Title IX where a teacher harasses a student without the knowledge of school administrators. Jane Doe, a thirteen year old student, had been sexually abused by a teacher, but there was no evidence that any school official was aware of the situation until after it ended. Instead of strict liability or theory of constructive notice, Doe relied on the familiar common law principle later applied by the Court in *Ellerth* and *Faragher* that an employer is vicariously liable for an employee's injurious actions, even if committed outside the scope of employment, if the employee "was aided in accomplishing the tort by the existence of the agency relationship."[121] According to this theory, the harasser's status as a teacher made his abuse possible by placing him in an authoritative position to take advantage of his adolescent student. Because teachers are almost always "aided" by the agency relationship, however, and application of the common law rule "would generate vicarious liability in virtually every case of teacher-student harassment," the Fifth Circuit rejected the approach in favor of its actual knowledge standard.

In a 5 to 4 opinion, the Supreme Court affirmed, avoiding any comparison to the strict liability and affirmative defense framework promulgated for Title VII employment law. It held that a student who has been sexually harassed by a teacher may not recover damages against the school district "unless an official of the school district who at a minimum has authority to institute corrective measures on the district's behalf has actual knowledge of, and is deliberately indifferent to, the teacher's misconduct."[122] The differing legislative constructs of Title VII and Title IX, and an apparent reluctance to impose excessive financial liability on schools, appeared to drive the Court's decision.

Unlike Title VII, Title IX has been judicially determined to provide only an "implied" private right of action and rather than a statute of general application, it imposes legal obligations only as a condition to the receipt of federal financial assistance. These distinctions persuaded the Court to "shape a sensible remedial scheme that best comports with the statute" and its legislative history.[123] In analyzing congressional intent, the Court examined the statutory provisions for Title IX enforcement by means of federal agency termination of federal funds to noncomplying school districts following notice and opportunity to be heard. Given the express notice requirement of the statute, the majority felt it unfair to impose a vicarious or constructive notice standard on school districts in private lawsuits. Moreover, there was concern that the award of damages in any given case might unfairly exceed the amount of federal funding actually received by the school. Consequently, there was no actionable Title IX claim since responsible school administrators were without notice or "actual knowledge" of the alleged sexual relationship. The Court summarily noted that Lago Vista's failure to promulgate and publicize an anti-harassment policy and grievance procedure, as mandated by U.S. Department of Education regulations, established neither actual notice, deliberate indifference, or even discrimination under Title IX.

Davis v. Monroe County Board of Education, decided in 1999, addressed the standard of liability that should be imposed on school districts to remedy student-on-student harassment.[124] The plaintiff in *Davis* alleged that her fifth-grade daughter had been harassed by another student over a prolonged period—a fact reported to teachers on several occasions—but that school officials had failed to take corrective action. A sharply divided Court determined that the plaintiff had stated a Title IX claim. Because the statute restricts the actions of federal grant recipients, however, and not the conduct of third parties, the Court again refused to impose vicarious liability on the school district. Instead, "a recipient of federal funds may be liable in damages under Title IX only for its own misconduct."[125] School authorities' own "deliberate indifference" to studenton-student harassment could violate Title IX in certain cases. Thus, the Court held, where officials have "actual knowledge" of the harassment, where the "harasser is under the school's disciplinary authority," and where the harassment is so severe "that it can be said to deprive the victims of access to the educational opportunities or benefits provided by the school," the district may be held liable for damages under Title IX.[126]

In qualifying the *Davis* standard, the Court suggested that student harassment may be far more difficult to prove than sexual harassment in employment. Beyond requiring "actual knowledge," the Court cautioned that "schools are unlike the adult workplace" and disciplinary decisions of school administrators are not to be "second guess[ed]" by lower courts unless "clearly unreasonable" under the circumstances. Additionally, the majority emphasized that "damages are not available for simple acts of teasing and name-calling among school children, even where these comments target differences in gender."[127] In effect, *Davis* left to school administrators the task of drawing the line between innocent teasing and actionable sexual harassment—a difficult and legally perilous task at best.

More recently, the Court issued a decision in *Fitzgerald v. Barnstable School Committee*,[128] a case in which the Court considered whether Title IX provides the exclusive statutory remedy for unlawful sex discrimination in the education context. The lower court, concluding that Title IX was the exclusive statutory remedy, had rejected a claim that the original plaintiffs filed under 42 U.S.C. §1983 for violations of Title IX and the Equal Protection Clause of the Constitution.[129] In a unanimous decision, the Court reversed, holding that "Title IX was not meant to be an exclusive mechanism for addressing gender discrimination in schools, or a substitute for § 1983 suits as a means of enforcing constitutional rights."[130] As a result, plaintiffs may file claims related to sex discrimination in education under both statutes in the future.

In 2001, OCR revised its Title IX guidance in light of Supreme Court decisions regarding school liability.[131] The guidance is intended to illustrate the principles that a school should use to recognize and effectively respond to sexual harassment of students in its program.

More recently, in the wake of several high-profile incidents involving student bullying, OCR released additional guidance that discusses when student bullying may violate federal education anti-discrimination laws and that clarifies a school's obligation to combat such bullying.[132] OCR also released separate guidance that specifically addresses the circumstances under which the harassment of gay students may be prohibited by law. Although discrimination on the basis of sexual orientation is not expressly forbidden by statute, in some cases, sexual orientation discrimination may also be a form of sex discrimination that violates Title IX.[133] As noted above, in the employment context, the Supreme Court has recognized that sex discrimination may encompass same-sex sexual harassment, meaning that sex discrimination is prohibited even if the harasser and victim are members of the same sex.[134] The Court has also ruled that gender stereotyping is a form of discrimination on the basis of sex.[135] Therefore, if a student who is gay is being harassed because of a failure to conform to gender stereotypes, such harassment is prohibited by Title IX. It is important to note, however, that Title IX prohibits sexual orientation discrimination only when it constitutes a form of sex discrimination. Thus, the statute may not prohibit all forms of sexual orientation discrimination or harassment of students.[136]

End Notes

[1] Title VII prohibits employment discrimination on the basis of race, color, religion, sex, or national origin. 42 U.S.C. §§2000e et seq.

[2] Title IX prohibits sex discrimination in federally funded education programs or activities. 20 U.S.C. §1681.

[3] 42 U.S.C. §2000e-2(a)(1).

[4] *Id.* at §§2000e et seq.

[5] 20 U.S.C. §§1681 et seq. See Franklin v. Gwinnet County Pub. Sch., 503 U.S. 60 (1992).

[6] See, e.g., Doe v. Taylor Indep. Sch. Dist., 975 F.2d 137 (5th Cir. 1992).

[7] For more details on agency guidance on sexual harassment, see the EEOC's website at http://www.eeoc.gov.

[8] 29 C.F.R. §1604.11(a).

[9] *Id.* at §1604.11.

[10] Equal Employment Opportunity Commission, Policy Guidance on Current Issues of Sexual Harassment, March 19, 1990, at http://www.eeoc.gov/policy/docs/currentissues.html.

[11] *Id.* at 405:6695.

[12] *Id.* at 405:6686.

[13] *Id.*

[14] Equal Employment Opportunity Commission, Enforcement Guidance: Vicarious Employer Liability for Unlawful Harassment by Supervisors, June 18, 1999, http://www.eeoc.gov/policy/docs/harassment.html.

[15] 413 F. Supp. 654, 657-58 (D.D.C. 1976).

[16] *Id.* at 660-61.

[17] 561 F.2d 983 (D.C.Cir. 1977).

[18] 568 F.2d 1044 (3d Cir. 1977).

[19] Karibian v. Columbia Univ., 14 F.3d 773, 777 (2d Cir.), cert. denied 512 U.S. 1213 (1994).

[20] 841 F.Supp 825 (N.D. Ill. 1994).

[21] 52 F.3d 543 (5th Cir. 1995).

[22] Bryson v. Chicago State Univ., 96 F.3d 912 (7th Cir. 1996). See also Durham Life Ins. Co. v. Evans, 166 F.3d 139, 153 (3d Cir. 1999).

[23] 151 F.3d 172, 175 (4th Cir. 1998).

[24] See Webb v. Cardiothoracic Surgery Assoc., 139 F.3d 532, 539 (5th Cir. 1998).

[25] Jones v. Clinton, 16 F. Supp. 2d 1054 (E.D.Ark. 1998).

[26] E.g., Cram v. Lamson & Sessions Co., 49 F.3d 466 (8th Cir. 1995); Sanders v. Casa View Baptist Church, 134 F.3d 331, 339 (5th Cir. 1998); Gary v. Long, 59 F.3d 1391, 1396 (D.C. Cir. 1995).

[27] Karibian v. Columbia Univ., supra n. 19. See also Jansen v. Packaging Corp of Am., 123 F.3d 490 (7th Cir. 1997).

[28] 524 U.S. 742 (1998).

[29] Under common law agency principles, the majority reasoned, an employer is generally immune from liability for the tortious conduct of its agent (the harassing supervisor in *Ellerth*), which is deemed to be "outside the scope of employment," unless the wrongdoer is "aided" in the harassment by "the existence of the agency relation." The "aided in the agency relation standard" differentiates supervisory harassment for which an employer may be automatically liable from similar acts committed by mere co-workers. And it is most clearly satisfied in those cases where the harassment culminates in a "tangible employment action."

[30] Ellerth, 524 U.S. 761.

[31] 641 F.2d 934 (1981).

[32] *Id.* at 945.

[33] 682 F.2d 897 (11th Cir. 1982). In an oft-quoted passage from its opinion, the court stated: Sexual harassment which creates a hostile or offensive environment for members of one sex is every bit the arbitrary barrier to sexual equality at the workplace that racial harassment is to racial equality. Surely, a requirement that a man or woman run a gauntlet of sexual abuse in return for the privilege of being allowed to work and make a living can be as demeaning and disconcerting as the harshest of racial epithets. A pattern of sexual harassment inflicted upon an employee because of her sex is a pattern of behavior that inflicts disparate treatment upon a member of one sex with respect to terms, conditions, or privileges of employment. There is no requirement that an employee subjected to such disparate treatment prove in addition that she suffered tangible job detriment. *Id.* at 902.

[34] 477 U.S. 57 (1986).

[35] *Id.* at 58.

[36] *Id.* at 62 (quoting *Henson v. Dundee*), supra n. 33 at 904. In *Meritor Savings* the complainant alleged that her supervisor demanded sexual relations over a three-year period, fondled her in front of other employees, followed her into the women's restroom and exposed himself to her, and forcibly raped her several times. She claimed she submitted for fear of jeopardizing her employment. During the period she received several promotions which, it was undisputed, were based on merit alone so that no exchange of job advancement for sexual favors (quid pro quo harassment) was alleged or found.

[37] *Id.* at 68 (citing 29 C.F.R. §1604.11(a)(1985)).

[38] *Id.* at 69.

[39] *Id.* at 72.

[40] Compare Rabidue v. Osceola Refining Co., 805 F.2d 611 (6th Cir. 1986); Scott v. Sears Roebuck, 798 F.2d 210 (7th Cir. 1986); and Brooms v. Regal Tube, 830 F.2d 1554 (11th Cir. 1987) with Andrews v. City of Philadelphia, 895 F.2d 1469 (3d Cir 1990); Burns v. McGregor Electronic Indus., Inc., 955 F.2d 559 (8th Cir. 1992); and Ellison v. Brady, 924 F.2d 872 (9th Cir. 1991).

[41] 510 U.S. 17 (1993).

[42] *Id.* at 21-22.

[43] *Id.* at 22-23.

[44] 760 F. Supp. 1486 (M.D.Fla. 1991).

[45] E.g. Highlander v. K.F.C. Nat'l Mgmt. Co., 805 F. 2d 644 (6th Cir. 1986); Waltman v. Int'l Paper Co., 875 F.2d 468, 475 (5th Cir. 1989); King v. Bd. of Regents, 898 F.2d 533, 537 (7th Cir. 1990). But cf. Vance v. Southern Tel. & Tel. Co., 863 F.2d 1503, 1510 (11th Cir. 1989).

[46] E.g. Cowan v. Prudential Ins. Co. of Am., 141 F.3d 751, 758 (7th Cir. 1998); Hall v. Gus Constr. Co., 842 F.2d 1010, 1017 (8th Cir. 1988); Jones v. Flagship Int'l, 793 F.2d 714 (5th Cir. 1986), cert. denied, 479 U.S. 1065 (1987).

[47] E.g. DeAngelis v. El Paso Officers' Ass'n, 51 F.3d 596 (5th Cir. 1995); Johnson v. County of Los Angeles Fire Dep't, 865 F. Supp, 1430, 1440 (C.D.Cal. 1994). But cf. O'Rourke v. City of Providence, 235 F.3d at 735-36; Aguilar v. Avis Rent A Car Sys., Inc., 21 Cal. 4th 121 (1999), cert. denied, 529 U.S. 1138 (2000).

[48] See Carter v. Chrysler Corp., 173 F.3d 693, 701 (8th Cir. 1999); Andrews v. City of Philadelphia, 898 F.2d 1469, 1485 (3d Cir. 1990); Bell v. Crackin Good Bakers, Inc., 777 F.2d 1497, 1503 (11th Cir. 1985); McKinney v. Dole, 765 F.2d 1129, 1138 (D.C.Cir. 1985). But cf. Brown v. Henderson, 257 F.3d 246 (2d Cir. 2001).

[49] See, e.g., Jones v. Wesco Inv. Inc., 846 F.2d 1154 n.5 (8th Cir. 1988); Swentek v. USAIR, Inc., 830 F.2d 552, 556 (4th Cir. 1987).

[50] Clark County Sch. Dist. v. Breeden, 532 U.S. 268 (2001). See also Scusa v. Nestle USA Co., 181 F.3d 958 (8th Cir. 1999); Lam v. Curators of the Univ. of Mo., 122 F.3d 654, 656-57 (8th Cir. 1997); Sprague v. Thorn Am., Inc, 129 F.3d 1355, 1366 (7th Cir. 1997); Saxton v. Am. Tel. & Tel. Co., 10 F.3d 526, 534 (7th Cir. 1993); Chamberlin v. 101 Realty, 915 F.2d 777 (1st Cir. 1990); Drinkwater v. Union Carbide Corp., 904 F.2d 853 (3d Cir. 1990); Ebert v. Lamar Truck Plaza, 878 F.2d 338 (10th Cir. 1989).

[51] Jones v. Clinton, 990 F. Supp. 657, 675-76 (D. Ark. 1998).

[52] McKensie v. Illinois Dep't of Transp., 92 F.3d 473, 478 (7th Cir. 1996). See also Butler v. Ysleta Indep. Sch. Dist., 161 F.3d 263 (5th Cir. 1998); Penry v. Fed. Home Loan Bank of Topeka, 155 F.3d 1257 (10th Cir. 1998). But cf. Abeita v. TransAm. Mailings, 159 F.3d 246 (6th Cir. 1998).

[53] E.g. Howley v. Town of Stratford, 217 F.3d 148 (2d Cir. 2000); Davis v. U.S. Postal Service, 142 F.3d 1334 (10th Cir. 1998); Crisonino v. New York City Hous. Auth., 985 F. Supp. 385 (S.D.N.Y. 1997).

[54] Equal Employment Opportunity Commission, Policy Guidance on Current Issues of Sexual Harassment, March 19, 1990, at http://www.eeoc.gov/policy/docs/currentissues.html.

[55] Ulane v. E. Airlines, Inc., 742 F.2d 1081 (7th Cir. 1984), cert. denied, 471 U.S. 1017 (1985).

[56] See, e.g., Yeary v. Goodwill Indus. - Knoxville, Inc., 107 F.3d 443 (6th Cir. 1997); Baskerville v. Culligan Int'l Co., 50 F.3d 428, 430 (7th Cir. 1995); Quick v. Donaldson Co., 90 F.3d 1372 (8th Cir. 1996).

[57] Garcia v. Elf Atochem N. Am., 28 F.3d 449 (5th Cir. 1994).

[58] 523 U.S. 75, 79 (1998).

[59] *Id.* at 80-81.

[60] *Id.* at 81.

[61] *Id.* at 81-82.

[62] See, e.g., Simonton v. Runyon, 232 F.3d 33 (2d Cir. 2000); Hamner v. St. Vincent Hosp. & Health Care Ctr., Inc., 224 F.3d 701 (7th Cir. 2000).

[63] Green v. Adm. of the Tulane Educ. Fund, 284 F.3d 642, 659 (5th Cir. 2002); Succar v. Dade County Sch. Bd., 229 F.3d 1343, 1345 (11th Cir. 2000).

[64] EEOC v. Nat'l Educ. Ass'n, 422 F.3d 840, 844 (9th Cir. 2005); DeClue v. Cent. Illinois Light Co., 223 F.3d 434, 437 (7th Cir. 2001).

[65] 202 Fed. Appx. 56 (6th Cir. 2006).

[66] *Id.* at 59.

[67] See, e.g., Vickers v. Fairfield Med. Ctr., 453 F.3d 757, 765 (6th Cir. 2006); Kay v. Independence Blue Cross, 142 Fed. Appx. 48 (3d Cir. 2005); Higgins v. New Balance Athletic Shoe Co., 194 F.3d 252 (1st Cir. 1999).

[68] 231 F.3d 1080 (7th Cir. 2000).

[69] Price Waterhouse v. Hopkins, 490 U.S. 228 (1989).

[70] 256 F.3d 864 (9th Cir. 2001). But cf., Kay v. Independence Blue Cross, 142 Fed. Appx. 48, 51 (3d Cir. 2005).

[71] 305 F.3d 1061 (9th Cir. 2002), cert. denied, MGM Grand Hotel, LLC v. Rene, 538 U.S. 922 (U.S. 2003).

[72] *Id.* at 1066.

[73] *Id.* at 1069.

[74] 168 F.3d 998 (7th Cir. 1999).

[75] La Day v. Catalyst Tech., Inc., 302 F.3d 474 (5th Cir. 2002).

[76] Dick v. Phone Directories Co., 397 F.3d 1256, 1264 (10th Cir. 2005).

[77] Civil Rights Act of 1991, P.L. 102-166, 105 Stat. 1071.

[78] E.g., Wirig v. Kinney Shoe Corp., 448 N.W. 2d 526, 51 FEP Cases 885 (Minn. Ct.App. 1989), aff'd in part and rev'd in part on other grounds, 461 N.W.2d 374 (Minn. Sup.Ct. 1990).

[79] See, e.g., Rojo v. Kliger, 52 Cal.3d 65, 901 P.2d 373 (Cal. Sup.Ct. 1990); Baker v. Weyerhauser Co., 903 F.2d 1342 (10th Cir. 1990); Syndex Corp. V. Dean, 820 S.W.2d 869 (Tex. App. 1991).

[80] 105 Stat. 1072, 42 U.S.C. §1981a.

[81] 42 U.S.C. §1981a(b)(3).

[82] *Id.* at §1981a(a)(1).

[83] *Id.* at §1981a(b)(1).

[84] *Id.* at §1981a(c).

[85] *Id.* at §1981a(b)(3).

[86] 532 U.S. 843 (2001).

[87] The Sixth Circuit in *Pollard* had held front pay subject to the cap, 213 F.2d 933, while other circuits had concluded to the contrary. E.g. Pals v. Schepel Buick & GMC Truck, Inc., 220 F.3d 495 (7th Cir. 2000); EEOC v. W&O Inc., 213 U.S. 600 (11th Cir. 2000).

[88] In a precursor to *Pollard*, for example, the Ninth Circuit affirmed a jury award of $350,000 in compensatory damages and $124,010.46 back pay for lost wages to a 59-year-old woman who was forced to quit her job due to posttraumatic stress syndrome caused by workplace harassment. Because she claimed that her age, stress, and background would foreclose a future job or career, the trial court also awarded the employee more than $600,000 in "front pay" to cover wages lost from the date of jury verdict forward for 11 years. Amtrak argued that this front pay award must be included in the $300,000 statutory cap on damages as "future pecuniary losses" specifically covered by the statute. Gotthardt v. Nat'l R.R., 191 F.3d 1148 (9th Cir. 1999).

[89] See Horn v. Duke Homes, 755 F.2d 599, 604 (7th Cir. 1985).

[90] Meritor Sav., 477 U.S. at 70-71.

[91] 524 U.S. 775 (1998).

[92] *Id.* at 803.

[93] *Id.* at 807-08.

[94] See, e.g., Murray v. Chicago Transit Auth., 252 F.3d 880 (7th Cir. 2001); Durham Life Ins. Co v. Evans, 166 F.3d 139, 153 (3d Cir. 1999); Watts v. Kroger Co., 170 F.3d 505, 510 (5th Cir. 1999); Sharp v. City of Houston, 164 F.3d 923 (5th Cir. 1999); Reinhold v. Commonwealth of Virginia, 151 F.3d 172 (4th Cir. 1998); Webb v. Cardiothoracic Surgery Assoc., 139 F.3d 532 (5th Cir. 1998).

[95] See, e.g., Durham Life Ins. Co., 166 F.3d at 162 (3d Cir. 1999); Sharp, 164 F.3d at 931-32; Wilson v. Tulsa Junior College, 164 F.3d 534 (10th Cir. 1998); But cf. Hall v. Bodine Elec. Co., 276 F.3d 345 (7th Cir. 2002).

[96] See Skidmore v. Precision Printing and Packaging, Inc., 188 F.3d 606 (5th Cir. 1999); Mockler v. Multnomah County, 140 F.3d 808 813 (9th Cir. 1998).

[97] See, e.g., Gawley v. Indiana Univ., 276 F.3d 301 (7th Cir. 2002); Jackson v. Arkansas Dep't of Educ., 272 F.3d 1020 (8th Cir. 2001); Indest v. Freeman Decorating, Inc., 164 F.3d 258 (5th Cir. 1999); Coates v. Sundor Brands, Inc., 164 F.3d 1361 (11th Cir. 1999); Van Zant v. KLM Royal Dutch Airlines, 80 F.3d 708, 715 (2d Cir. 1996); Steiner v. Showboat Operating Co., 25 F.3d 1459 (9th Cir. 1994), cert. denied, 513 U.S. 1082 (1995).

[98] See, e.g., Cotran v. Rollins Hudig Hall Int'l, Inc., 17 Cal. 4th 93 (1998); Morrow v. Wal-Mart Stores, Inc., 152 F.3d 559 (7th Cir. 1998); Waggoner v. City of Garland Tex., 987 F.2d 1160, 1165 (5th Cir. 1993).

[99] See, e.g., McKenzie v. Illinois Dep't of Transp., 92 F.3d 473 (7th Cir. 1996).

[100] See, e.g., Farley v. Am. Cast Iron Pipe Co., 115 F.3d 1548 (11th Cir. 1997); Gary v. Long, 59 F. 3d 1391 (D.C. Cir 1995).

[101] 527 U.S. 526 (1999).

[102] 542 U.S. 129 (2004).

[103] Ellerth, 524 U.S. at 761.

[104] Jaros v. Lodge Net Enter. Corp., 294 F.3d 960 (8th Cir. 2002).

[105] Turner v. Dowbrands, Inc., No. 99-3984, 2000 U.S. App. LEXIS 15733 (6th Cir. 2002); Caridad v. Metro-North Commuter R.R., 191 F.3d 283 (2d Cir. 1999), cert. denied, 529 U.S. 1107 (2000).

[106] Suders, 542 U.S. at 140-141.

[107] *Id.* at 209.

[108] Lissau v. S. Food Serv., 159 F.3d 177, 181 (4th Cir. 1998); Wathen v. GE, 115 F.3d 400, 405 (6th Cir. 1997); Dici v. Pennsylvania, 91 F.3d 542, 552 (3d Cir. 1996); Haynes v. Williams, 88 F.3d 898 (10th Cir. 1996); Tomka v. Seiler Corp., 66 F.3d 1295 (2d Cir. 1995); EEOC v. AIC Sec. Investigations, Ltd., 55 F.3d 1276 (7th Cir. 1995); Gary v. Long, 59 F.3d 1391 (D.C. Cir. 1995), cert. denied, 516 U.S. 1011 (1995); Grant v. Loan Star Co., 21 F.3d 649 (5th Cir. 1994), cert. denied, 513 U.S. 1015 (1994); Miller v. Maxwell's Int'l Inc., 991 F.2d 583 (9th Cir. 1993), cert. denied, 510 U.S. 1109 (1994); Busby v. City of Orlando, 931 F.2d 764 (11th Cir. 1991).

[109] 42 U.S.C. §2000e-3(a).

[110] 548 U.S. 53 (2006).

[111] *Id.* at 57.

[112] 555 U.S. 271 (2008).

[113] *Id.* at 849.

[114] In a related development in a Title VII case that involved allegations of sex discrimination but not sexual harassment, the Court determined that Title VII protects third parties who have not personally engaged in protected activity from retaliation by employers. Thompson v. N. Am. Stainless, LP, 131 S. Ct. 863 (2011).

[115] 20 U.S.C. §1681(a).

[116] 34 C.F.R. §100.7(d)(1)(1995).

[117] 441 U.S. 677 (1979).

[118] A private right of action allows an individual to sue in court for violations under a statute rather than wait for a federal agency to pursue a complaint administratively.

[119] 503 U.S. 60 (1992).

[120] 524 U.S. 274 (1998).

[121] Doe v. Lago Vista Indep. Sch. Dist., 106 F.3d 1223, 1225 (5th Cir. 1997) (citing Restatement (Second) of Agency §219(2)(d)(1958)).

[122] Gebser, 524 U.S. at 277 (1998).

[123] *Id.* at 284.

[124] 526 U.S. 629 (1999). Prior to *Davis*, the federal appeals courts were divided between those that refused to award Title IX damages or injunctive relief against a school district for student-on-student or "peer" sexual harassment, Rowinsky v. Bryan Indep. Sch. Dist., 80 F.3d 1006 (5th Cir.), cert. denied 519 U.S. 861 (1996), Davis v. Monroe, 120 F.3d 1390 (11th Cir. 1997), and others that had applied agency principles and Title VII legal standards to hold school officials liable for failure to take reasonable steps to prevent known hostile environment harassment by students or other third parties. Murray v. New York Univ. Coll. of Dentistry, 57 F.3d 243, 248-50 (2d Cir. 1995); Brown v. Hot, Sexy and Safer Prod., Inc., 68 F.3d 525, 540 (1st Cir. 1995), cert. denied 516 U.S. 1159 (1996); and Clyde K. v. Puyallup Sch. Dist., 35 F.3d 1396, 1402 (9th Cir. 1994).

[125] Davis, 526 U.S. at 640.

[126] *Id.* at 650.

[127] *Id.* at 652.

[128] 555 U.S. 246 (2008).

[129] 42 U.S.C. §1983, which provides a remedy for deprivation of rights under color of state law, creates no new substantive rights but rather provides relief where state law is inadequate. Thus, individuals who sue under §1983 must find a source of rights elsewhere. As a result, §1983 is often used to enforce constitutional rights, such as the right to equal protection.

[130] Fitzgerald, 555 U.S. at 258.

[131] Department of Education, Revised Sexual Harassment Guidance: Harassment of Students By School Employees, Other Students, or Third Parties, January 19, 2001, at http://www.ed.gov/about/offices/list/ocr/docs/shguide.html.

[132] United States Department of Education, *Office for Civil Rights*, Dear Colleague Letter, October 26, 2010, http://www2.ed.gov/about/offices/list/ocr/letters/colleague-201010.html.

[133] *See, e.g.*, Ray v. Antioch Unified Sch. Dist., 107 F. Supp. 2d 1165 (N.D. Cal. 2000); Doe v. Perry Cmty. Sch. Dist., 316 F. Supp. 2d 809 (S.D. Iowa 2004).

[134] Oncale v. Sundowner Offshore Servs., 523 U.S. 75 (1998).

[135] Price Waterhouse v. Hopkins, 490 U.S. 228 (1989).

[136] For more information on sexual harassment in schools, see OCR's policy guidance on the issue. U.S. Department of Education, *Office for Civil Rights*, Revised Sexual Harassment Guidance: Harassment of Students By School Employees, Other Students, or Third Parties, January 2001, http://www2.ed.gov/about/offices/list/ocr/docs/ shguide.html#Guidance.

In: Sex Discrimination and Harassment   ISBN 978-1-62257-466-7
Editors: H. Andrews and S. Spencer   © 2012 Nova Science Publishers, Inc.

Chapter 2

SEX DISCRIMINATION AND THE UNITED STATES SUPREME COURT: DEVELOPMENTS IN THE LAW[*]

Jody Feder

SUMMARY

In its sex discrimination decisions, the United States Supreme Court not only has defined the applicability of the equal protection guarantees of the Constitution and the nondiscriminatory policies of federal statutes, but also has rejected the use of gender stereotypes and has continued to recognize the discriminatory effect of gender hostility in the workplace and in schools. This report focuses on sex discrimination challenges based on: the equal protection guarantees of the Fourteenth and Fifth Amendments; the prohibition against employment discrimination contained in Title VII of the Civil Rights Act of 1964; and the prohibition against sex discrimination in education contained in Title IX of the Education Amendments of 1972. Although this report focuses on recent legal developments in each of these areas, this report also provides historical context by discussing selected landmark sex discrimination cases.

Despite the fact that the Court's analysis of sex discrimination challenges under the Constitution differs from its analysis of sex

---

[*] This is an edited, reformatted and augmented version of Congressional Research Service, Publication No. RL30253, dated January 6, 2012.

discrimination under the two federal statutes discussed in this report, it is apparent that the Court is willing to refine its standards of review under both schemes to accommodate the novel claims presented by these cases. The Court's decisions in cases involving Title VII and Title IX are particularly noteworthy because they illustrate the Court's recognition of sexual harassment in both the workplace and the classroom.

During the recent 2010-2011 term, the Court issued rulings in two high-profile cases involving claims of sex discrimination in employment. In *Thompson v. North American Stainless*, which involved a retaliation claim by a man who was fired three weeks after his then-fiancée filed a sex discrimination complaint, the Court determined that Title VII of the Civil Rights Act protects third parties who have not personally engaged in protected activity from retaliation by employers. In *Wal-Mart Store v. Dukes*, the Court rejected class action status for current and former female Wal-Mart employees who allege that the company has engaged in discrimination regarding pay and promotions.

INTRODUCTION

In its sex discrimination decisions, the United States Supreme Court not only has defined the applicability of the equal protection guarantees of the Constitution and the nondiscriminatory policies of federal statutes, but also has rejected the use of gender stereotypes and has continued to recognize the discriminatory effect of gender hostility in the workplace and in schools. This report focuses on sex discrimination challenges based on the equal protection guarantees of the Fourteenth and Fifth Amendments;[1] the prohibition against employment discrimination contained in Title VII of the Civil Rights Act of 1964;[2] and the prohibition against sex discrimination in education contained in Title IX of the Education Amendments of 1972.[3] Although this report focuses on recent legal developments in each of these areas, this report also provides historical context by discussing selected landmark sex discrimination cases.

EQUAL PROTECTION CASES

Constitutional challenges that allege discrimination on the basis of sex are premised either on the equal protection guarantees of the Fourteenth Amendment or the equal protection component of the Fifth Amendment. To maintain an equal protection challenge, government action must be established; that is, it must be shown that the government, and not a private actor, has acted in a discriminatory manner. While the Fourteenth Amendment prohibits discriminatory conduct by the states, the Fifth Amendment forbids such action by the federal government.

The Fourteenth Amendment provides, in relevant part: "No state shall make or enforce any law which shall abridge the privileges or immunities of the citizens of the United States; nor shall any State deprive any person of life, liberty, or property, without due process of law; *nor deny to any person within its jurisdiction the equal protection of the laws*."[4]

Although the Fourteenth Amendment requires equal protection, it does not preclude the classification of individuals. The Court has noted that the Constitution does not require things which are "different in fact or opinion to be treated in law as though they were the same."[5] A classification will not offend the Constitution unless it is characterized by invidious discrimination.[6] The Court has adopted three levels of review to establish the presence of invidious discrimination:

1) Strict scrutiny. This most active form of judicial review has been applied where there is either a suspect classification, such as race, national origin, or alienage, or a burdening of a fundamental interest such as privacy or marriage. A classification will survive strict scrutiny if the government can show that it is *necessary* to achieving a *compelling* interest.[7] Generally, statutory classifications subject to strict scrutiny are invalidated.

2) Intermediate scrutiny. This level of review is not as rigorous as strict scrutiny. A classification will survive intermediate scrutiny if it is *substantially related* to achieving an *important* government objective.[8] Sex classifications are subject to intermediate scrutiny.

3) Rational basis review. This least active form of judicial review allows a classification to survive an equal protection challenge if the classification is *rationally related* to a *legitimate* government interest.[9] This level of review is characterized by its deference to legislative judgment. Most economic regulations are subject to rational basis review.

The Court's adoption of intermediate scrutiny for sex classifications did not occur until 1976. In *Craig v. Boren*, the Court declared unconstitutional an Oklahoma statute that prohibited the sale of "nonintoxicating" 3.2% beer to males under the age of 21 and to females under the age of 18.[10] Females between the ages of 18 and 21, however, were allowed to purchase 3.2% beer.

Although the Court agreed with the state's argument that the protection of public health and safety is an important government interest, it found that the gender classification employed by the statute was not substantially related to achieving that goal. The statistical evidence presented by the state to show that more 18 to 20-year-old males were arrested for drunk driving and that males between the ages of 17 and 21 were overrepresented among those injured in traffic accidents could not establish that the statute's gender classification was substantially related to ensuring public health and safety.

In establishing an intermediate level of review for sex classifications, the *Craig* Court identified what has been a common theme in sex discrimination cases under the Fourteenth Amendment: stereotypes and generalizations about the sexes.[11] In *Craig*, the Court acknowledged its previous invalidation of statutes that premised their classifications on misconceptions concerning the role of females. The Court's rejection of the use of stereotypes may be seen in many of the cases in this area.[12] The Court's more recent decisions similarly allude to the use of stereotypes and generalizations.

For example, in *J.E.B. v. Alabama*, the Court determined that the state could not use its peremptory challenges to exclude male jurors in a paternity and child support action.[13] In reaching its conclusion, the Court reviewed the historical exclusion of women from juries because of the belief that women were "too fragile and virginal to withstand the polluted courtroom atmosphere."[14] In *J.E.B.*, the Court questioned the state's generalizations of male jurors being more sympathetic to the arguments of a father in a paternity action and female jurors being more receptive to the mother. The Court maintained that state actors who exercise peremptory challenges in reliance on gender stereotypes "ratify and reinforce prejudicial views of the relative abilities of men and women."[15] The Court feared that this discriminatory use of peremptory challenges not only would raise questions about the fairness of the entire proceeding, but also would create the impression that the judicial system had acquiesced in the denial of participation by one gender.

In *U.S. v. Virginia*, the Court conducted a more searching form of intermediate scrutiny to find unconstitutional the exclusion of women from the Virginia Military Institute (VMI).[16] Although the Court reiterated that a classification must be substantially related to an important government interest, the Court also required the state to establish an "exceedingly persuasive justification" for its actions.[17]

Virginia advanced two arguments in support of VMI's exclusion of women: first, the single-sex education offered by VMI contributed to a diversity of educational approaches in Virginia; second, VMI employed a unique adversative method of training that would be destroyed if women were admitted.

After reviewing the history of Virginia's educational system, the Court concluded that VMI was not established or maintained to promote educational diversity. In fact, VMI's "historic and constant plan" was to offer a unique educational benefit to only men,[18] rather than to complement other Virginia institutions by providing a single-sex educational option. Further, the Court recognized Virginia's historic reluctance to allow women to pursue higher education. Any interest Virginia had in maintaining educational diversity seemed to be "proffered in response to litigation."[19]

In addressing Virginia's second argument, the Court expressed concern over the exclusion of women from VMI because of generalizations about their ability. While acknowledging that most women would probably not choose the adversative method, the Court maintained that some women had the will and capacity to succeed at VMI. Following *J.E.B.*, the Court cautioned state actors not to rely on overbroad generalizations to perpetuate patterns of discrimination. While the Court believed that the adversative method did promote important goals, it concluded that the exclusion of women was not substantially related to achieving those goals.

After determining that VMI's exclusion of women violated the Fourteenth Amendment, the Court reviewed the state's remedy, a separate program for women. Virginia established the Virginia Women's Institute for Leadership (VWIL) following the adverse decision of the court of appeals. Unlike VMI, VWIL did not use the adversative method because it was believed to be inappropriate for most women,[20] and VWIL lacked the faculty, facilities, and course offerings available at VMI. Because VWIL was not a comparable single-sex institution for women, the Court concluded that it was an inadequate remedy for the state's equal protection violations. VMI subsequently became coeducational.

The Court's most recent equal protection pronouncements with respect to sex discrimination both involved immigration issues. In *Miller v. Albright*, the Court considered a challenge to §309 of the Immigration and Nationality Act.[21] The petitioner, the child of an American father and a Filipino mother, contended that §309 imposed additional requirements for establishing American citizenship when a child is fathered by an American citizen outside of the United States.[22] For children born of a citizen mother and an alien father, citizenship is established at birth. However, for children born of a citizen father and an alien mother, citizenship is not established until the father or the child takes affirmative steps to confirm their relationship by the child's eighteenth birthday. In this case, the petitioner's father did not attempt to establish his relationship with his daughter until after her eighteenth birthday. Thus, the petitioner's application for citizenship was denied.

The case produced five different opinions. While six justices agreed that the petitioner's complaint should be dismissed, they provided different reasons for this conclusion. Justices Stevens and Rehnquist contended that the petitioner's complaint lacked merit, maintaining that §309's distinction between "illegitimate" children of U.S. citizen mothers and "illegitimate" children of U.S. citizen fathers is permissible under heightened scrutiny because it is "eminently reasonable and justified by important Government policies."[23] Justices O'Connor and Kennedy contended, however, that the distinction could withstand only rational basis review and should not satisfy the kind of heightened scrutiny Justice Stevens seemed to conduct. Setting aside the issue of §309's constitutionality, Justices O'Connor and Kennedy believed that the petitioner lacked the standing necessary to even pursue her claim. Finally, Justices Scalia and Thomas contended that the petitioner's complaint should be dismissed because the Court lacks the power to confer citizenship. Having acknowledged that Congress has the exclusive authority to grant citizenship, Justices Scalia and Thomas believed that there was no need to address the constitutionality of §309. Justices Ginsburg, Breyer, and Souter dissented in opinions written by Justices Ginsburg and Breyer.

In their separate opinions, Justices Stevens, O'Connor, Ginsburg, and Breyer each addressed the petitioner's argument that §309 invokes gender stereotypes. The petitioner contended that §309 relies on the belief that an American father "remains aloof from day-to-day child rearing duties," and will not be as close to his child.[24] Justice Stevens, however, maintained that the statute has a non-stereotypical purpose of ensuring the existence of a blood relationship between father and child. Justice Stevens recognized that the distinction is reasonable because mothers have the opportunity to establish parentage at birth, while fathers do not always have that opportunity. Further, he contended that the distinction encourages the development of a healthy relationship between the citizen father and the foreign-born child, and fosters ties between the child and the United States. Thus, §309's additional requirements are appropriate for fathers, but unnecessary for mothers.

In their dissenting opinions, Justices Ginsburg and Breyer contended that §309 relies on generalizations about men and women and the ties they maintain with their children. Justice Ginsburg argued that §309's goals of assuring ties between the citizen father and the foreign-born child, and between the child and the United States can be achieved without reference to gender, while Justice Breyer argued similarly, positing a distinction between caretaker and non-caretaker parents, rather than mother and father.

In *Nguyen v. INS*, the Court considered a second challenge to §309.[25] The facts in *Nguyen* closely resembled those in *Miller*. Nguyen, the child of a citizen father and a non-citizen mother, born out of wedlock, challenged §309 on the grounds that its differing requirements for acquiring citizenship, based on the sex of the citizen parent, violated the Fifth Amendment's guarantee of equal protection.

A majority of the Court concluded that §309's differing requirements were justified by two important government objectives. First, the Court found that the government has an important interest in assuring that a biological parent-child relationship exists.[26] While a mother's relationship to a child may be established at birth or from hospital records, a father may not be present at the birth and may not be included on such records. In this way, the Court maintained, fathers and mothers are not similarly situated with regard to establishing biological parenthood.[27] Thus, a "different set of rules ... is neither surprising nor troublesome from a constitutional perspective."[28]

Second, the Court found that the government has an important government interest in ensuring that the child and the citizen parent have some demonstrated opportunity or potential to develop a relationship "that consists of the real, everyday ties that provide a connection between child and citizen parent and, in turn, the United States."[29] The opportunity for a meaningful relationship is presented to the mother at birth. However, the father is not assured of a similar opportunity. The Court concluded that §309 ensures that an opportunity for a meaningful relationship is presented to the father before citizenship is conferred upon his child.

As a result, the Court found that §309's differing requirements were substantially related to the important government interests. The Court noted that by linking citizenship to the child's youth, Congress promoted an opportunity for a parent-child relationship during the formative years of the child's life.[30] Alluding to its decision in *VMI*, the Court maintained that the fit between the §309 requirements and the important government interests was "exceedingly persuasive."[31]

Like the petitioner in *Miller*, Nguyen argued that §309 embodied a gender-based stereotype. However, the Court found that §309 addresses an "undeniable difference in the circumstance of the parents at the time a child is born."[32] This difference is not the result of a stereotype or "a frame of mind resulting from irrational or uncritical analysis."[33] Rather, §309 recognizes simply that at the moment of birth, the mother's knowledge of the child is established in a way not guaranteed to the unwed father.

While the Court's recent decisions involving sex and equal protection illustrate that it is concerned with the stereotyping of men and women, it is unclear whether it will continue to subject sex classifications and any related stereotypes to a traditional form of intermediate scrutiny. The Court's requirement of an "exceedingly persuasive justification" in *VMI* suggests that it may be interested in conducting a more exacting form of judicial review for sex classifications. In his *Miller* dissent, Justice Breyer emphasized the need to apply the standard established in *VMI*. However, in *Nguyen*, both the majority and the dissenting justices, in discussing an "exceeding persuasive justification," simply reiterated the traditional test that is used when applying intermediate scrutiny.[34] Thus, it is not clear whether sex classifications in future cases will be subject to a traditional form of intermediate scrutiny or some form of heightened scrutiny.

TITLE VII OF THE CIVIL RIGHTS ACT OF 1964

Title VII prohibits an employer from discriminating against any individual with respect to hiring or the terms and conditions of employment because of such individual's race, color, religion, sex, or national origin.[35] Title VII applies to a broad range of employment practices, including discrimination because of sex in hiring, placement, promotion, demotion, transfer, termination, and discipline. Because the statute prohibits sex discrimination with respect to all terms and conditions of employment, discrimination regarding salary, leave, and other benefits may also violate the act. In addition, the statute prohibits discrimination in referrals by employment agencies, actions by unions, and retaliation against employees for filing or participating in a Title VII claim or for opposing an employer's discriminatory practices. Title VII contains several exceptions to the prohibition against sex discrimination, the most important of which permits otherwise discriminatory conduct that satisfies a bona fide occupational qualification (BFOQ). Under §703(e)(1) of Title VII, an employer may discriminate on the basis of "religion, sex, or national origin in those certain instances where religion, sex, or national origin is a bona fide occupational qualification reasonably necessary to the normal operation of that particular business or enterprise."[36]

Although a wide variety of Title VII sex discrimination claims have been litigated in the courts, the major Supreme Court sex discrimination cases under

Title VII have primarily focused on the following issues: pregnancy discrimination, gender stereotypes, mixed motives, sexual harassment, employer liability, retaliation, and class action status. These issues, as well as a discussion of the two different types of discrimination recognized under Title VII, are described below.

Disparate Treatment and Disparate Impact

The Court has developed two principal models for proving claims of employment discrimination. The "disparate treatment" model focuses on an employer's intent to discriminate. Alternately, the "disparate impact" model is concerned with the adverse effects of an employer's practices on a protected class. Under disparate impact analysis, a facially neutral employment practice may violate Title VII even if there is no evidence of an employer's intent to discriminate. To succeed, a plaintiff must demonstrate that the application of a specific employment practice has had a different effect on a particular group of employees.[37]

Both disparate treatment and disparate impact analyses involve a system of evidentiary burden shifting. Both models require the plaintiff to establish a prima facie case of discrimination.[38] If such a case can be established, the burden shifts to the employer to articulate a defense for its actions. For example, the employer may produce evidence showing that its actions are justified because of the needs of its business. Ultimately, however, the plaintiff retains the burden of persuasion; that is, the plaintiff must establish that the employer's assertion of a legitimate, nondiscriminatory reason for its actions was a pretext to obscure unlawful discrimination.[39]

Pregnancy Discrimination

In recent years, the Court has addressed Title VII and sex discrimination most frequently in the context of sexual harassment. In *UAW v. Johnson Controls*, however, the Court considered whether an employer may discriminate against fertile women because of its interest in protecting potential fetuses.[40]

Johnson Controls, a battery manufacturer, implemented a policy that excluded "women who are pregnant or who are capable of bearing children" from jobs that exposed them to lead,[41] which was the primary ingredient in the manufacturing process at Johnson Controls. Although fertile women were excluded from employment, fertile men were still permitted to work.

The Court found that Johnson Controls' policy was facially discriminatory because it did not apply to the reproductive capacity of the company's male employees in the same way it applied to that of female employees. The Court's conclusion was bolstered by the Pregnancy Discrimination Act of 1978 (PDA), which provides that discrimination "on the basis of sex" for purposes of violating Title VII includes discrimination "because of or on the basis of pregnancy, childbirth, or related medical conditions."[42]

Although Johnson Controls asserted that sex was a BFOQ for protecting fetal safety, the Court maintained that discrimination on the basis of sex for safety concerns is allowed only in narrow circumstances.[43] The Court stressed that to qualify as a BFOQ, an employment practice must relate to the essence or central mission of the employer's business.[44]

Because reproductive capacity does not interfere with a woman's ability to perform work related to battery manufacturing, the Court rejected Johnson Controls' BFOQ defense.

In 2009, the Supreme Court issued a decision in *AT&T v. Hulteen*,[45] a pregnancy discrimination case that involved questions about whether women who took maternity leave before the PDA went into effect were entitled to protection. Prior to enactment of the PDA, AT&T had calculated pension benefits based on a seniority system that considered years of service minus uncredited leave, but had given less leave credit for pregnancy absences than for other types of medical leave.

The plaintiffs claimed that, for purposes of calculating their current retirement and other benefits, they were entitled to retroactive credit for the time they spent on maternity leave, while the employer argued that they were not required to account for leave that took place before the PDA went into effect.

Ultimately, the Court ruled in favor of AT&T, ruling that its seniority system did not violate Title VII "when it gives current effect to such rules that operated before the PDA."[46] Under Title VII, it is not unlawful for an employer to provide different levels of benefits pursuant to a bona fide seniority system, as long as there is no intention to discriminate.[47]

According to the Court, AT&T's pre-PDA seniority system did not reflect intentional sex discrimination because it was lawful at the time it was adopted. Therefore, the Court held that AT&T's pension calculations were made pursuant to a bona fide seniority system and were permissible under the statute.

Gender Stereotypes

The Supreme Court has also ruled that employment decisions made on the basis of gender stereotypes may constitute unlawful sex discrimination. In *Price Waterhouse v. Hopkins*,[48] the plaintiff, a woman who was denied partnership in the accounting firm where she worked, was apparently rejected because of concerns about her interpersonal skills. Some of these concerns, however, appeared to reflect gender stereotypes. For example, one male partner referred to the plaintiff as "macho," and another informed her that she could improve her chances of making partner if she learned to "walk more femininely, talk more femininely, dress more femininely, wear make-up, have her hair styled, and wear jewelry."[49] Reasoning that sex stereotyping is a form of discrimination on the basis of sex, the Court found that employment decisions that result from sex stereotypes may violate Title VII.[50]

Although the decision was in part a victory for employees who have been victims of employment actions based on gender stereotypes, another aspect of the *Hopkins* ruling favored employers by requiring a lower standard of proof when employers defend their actions in mixed-motive cases. In mixed-motive cases such as *Hopkins*, there are both legitimate and illegitimate reasons for an employer's adverse employment action. In such cases, the Court held that employers may rebut an employee's showing that discrimination was a "motivating factor" in the adverse action by proving that they would have made the same decision even if discrimination had not been a factor. This holding made it easier for employers to defend against discrimination lawsuits by their employees.

Mixed Motives

As noted above, a mixed-motive employment discrimination case is a case in which the employer has both legitimate and illegitimate reasons for taking the challenged employment action. Several years after the Supreme Court ruled in the *Hopkins* case, Congress passed Title VII amendments that partially overturned the decision.[51] In the amendments, Congress added a provision that defined unlawful employment actions to include situations in which discrimination is "a motivating factor for any employment practice, even though other factors also motivated the practice."[52] If an employer violates this provision but establishes that it would have taken the same employment action absent the illegitimate motive, the amendments specify that courts may grant the plaintiff declaratory and injunctive relief, as well as attorneys' fees, although plaintiffs are not entitled to damages, hiring, reinstatement, or promotion.[53]

The Title VII amendments, however, did not address certain questions regarding the evidentiary burden of proof in mixed-motive cases. In 2003, the Supreme Court addressed the issue, ruling in *Desert Palace v. Costa* that direct evidence of discrimination is not required in mixed-motive cases.[54] By allowing plaintiffs to present circumstantial evidence of discrimination, the decision made it easier for employees to win in mixed-motive cases.

Sexual Harassment

Courts have recognized two forms of sexual harassment under Title VII. The first, quid pro quo sexual harassment, occurs when submission to unwelcome sexual advances or other conduct of a sexual nature is made a condition of an individual's employment or is otherwise used as the basis for employment decisions. The second form of harassment involves conduct that has the purpose or effect of interfering unreasonably with an individual's work performance or of creating a hostile or offensive working environment. This second form of sexual harassment, which the Court first recognized as a cognizable claim in *Meritor Savings Bank, FSB v. Vinson*,[55] is referred to as "hostile environment" sexual harassment.

In *Harris v. Forklift Systems, Inc.*, the Court sought to define when a workplace was sufficiently "hostile" for purposes of maintaining a claim under Title VII.[56] The petitioner, a female manager at an equipment rental company, alleged that the company's president created a hostile environment by repeatedly insulting her because of her gender and making her the target of unwanted sexual innuendos.

The Court determined that an employee does not need to suffer injury to assert a hostile environment claim under Title VII: "So long as the environment would reasonably be perceived, and is perceived, as hostile or abusive ... there is no need for it also to be psychologically injurious."[57] The Court identified four factors that should be considered to determine whether a hostile environment exists: (1) the frequency of the discriminatory conduct; (2) the severity of such conduct; (3) whether the conduct is physically threatening or humiliating; and (4) whether the conduct interferes unreasonably with an employee's work performance.[58] Although the Court recognized these factors as those to be considered in identifying a hostile environment, it emphasized that no single factor is determinative.

Same-Sex Sexual Harassment

In 1998, the Court interpreted Title VII's prohibition against discrimination "because of ... sex" to include harassment involving a plaintiff and defendant of the same sex.[59] The petitioner in *Oncale v. Sundowner Offshore Services, Inc.* alleged that he was physically assaulted in a sexual manner and was threatened with rape by three male co-workers.[60] Two of the co-workers had supervisory authority over the petitioner.

Although the Court acknowledged that Congress was "assuredly" not concerned with male-onmale sexual harassment when it enacted Title VII, it found no justification in the statutory language or the Court's precedents for excluding same-sex harassment claims from the coverage of Title VII.[61] At the same time, the Court stated that inquiries in same-sex harassment cases require careful consideration of the social context in which particular behavior occurs and is experienced by the claimant. For example, the Court distinguished a football player being patted on the butt in a locker room from similar behavior occurring in an office. The Court contended that this kind of consideration would prevent Title VII from becoming a "general civility code" for the American workplace.[62]

Employer Liability

The Court continued its examination of hostile environment sexual harassment in two cases involving vicarious liability. In *Faragher v. City of Boca Raton*, the Court found that an employer is vicariously liable for actionable discrimination caused by a supervisor, subject to an affirmative defense that must consider the reasonableness of the employer's conduct, as well as the conduct of the employee.[63] The petitioner, a former lifeguard for the Marine Safety Section of Boca Raton's Parks and Recreation Department, alleged that she was subject to an environment characterized by lewd remarks, gender-biased speech, and uninvited and offensive touching by her former supervisors.

Recognizing that the authority conferred as a result of a supervisor's relationship with the employer allows the supervisor greater ability to act inappropriately, the Court concluded that an employer could be vicariously liable when a supervisor misuses that authority. As the Court noted, "When a person with supervisory authority discriminates in the terms and conditions of subordinates' employment, his actions necessarily draw upon his superior position over the people who report to him ... whereas an employee generally cannot check a supervisor's abusive conduct the same way that she might deal with abuse from a co-worker."[64]

While the Court recognized that there could be vicarious liability for the misuse of supervisory authority, it established the availability of an affirmative defense for employers. Under this affirmative defense, an employer could assert that it exercised reasonable care to prevent and correct any sexually harassing behavior or establish that the employee unreasonably failed to take advantage of any preventive or corrective opportunities provided by the employer. The Court believed that the employer's ability to assert such an affirmative defense was consistent with Title VII's objective of encouraging employers to prevent sexual harassment from occurring.[65]

After applying its new rules to the case at bar, the Court concluded that the city did not exercise reasonable care to prevent the supervisors' harassing conduct. Although the city maintained a policy against sexual harassment, it failed to disseminate that policy to beach employees. Further, the city made no attempt to monitor the conduct of the supervisors or assure employees that they could bypass harassing supervisors to register complaints.

The Court revisited the issue of vicarious liability for employers in *Burlington Industries v. Ellerth*, a companion case to *Faragher*.[66] In *Ellerth*, the Court maintained that an employer may be found vicariously liable for harassment by a supervisor even if the employee suffers no adverse, tangible job consequences.

The petitioner in *Ellerth* alleged that she was subjected to repeated offensive remarks and gestures by a mid-level manager who supervised the petitioner's immediate supervisor. On three occasions, the manager made remarks that could be construed as threats to deny the petitioner job benefits. For example, the manager encouraged the petitioner to "loosen up" because he "could make [her] life very hard or very easy at Burlington."[67] Although Burlington maintained a policy against sexual harassment, the petitioner did not inform anyone in authority about the manager's misconduct. Instead, the petitioner resigned from her position, providing reasons unrelated to the harassment. Three weeks after her resignation, the petitioner informed Burlington of her true reasons for leaving.

While the manager's threats suggested that the claim should be analyzed as a quid pro quo claim, the Court categorized it as a hostile environment claim because it involved only unfulfilled threats. After reviewing the petitioner's claim in terms similar to *Faragher*, the Court determined that the manager at Burlington also misused his supervisory authority. The Court concluded that Burlington should be given the opportunity to assert and prove an affirmative defense to liability.

The Court has also addressed the availability of punitive damages for violations of Title VII. In *Kolstad v. American Dental Association*,[68] the Court continued to build on its holdings in *Faragher* and *Ellerth* by concluding that although an employer may be vicariously liable for the misconduct of its supervisory employees, it will not be subject to punitive damages if it has made good faith efforts to comply with Title VII. The Court noted that subjecting employers that adopt antidiscrimination policies to punitive damages would undermine Title VII's objective of encouraging employers to prevent discrimination in the workplace.

In 2004, the Supreme Court considered the defenses, if any, that may be available to an employer against an employee's claim that she was forced to resign because of "intolerable" sexual harassment at the hands of a supervisor. As noted above, an employer may generally assert an affirmative defense to supervisory harassment under the Court's 1998 rulings in *Faragher* and *Ellerth*. The defense is not available, however, if the harassment includes a "tangible employment action," such as discharge or demotion. In *Pennsylvania State Police v. Suders*,[69] the plaintiff claimed the tangible adverse action was supervisory harassment so severe that it drove the employee to quit, a constructive discharge in effect. The Court, in an opinion by Justice Ginsburg, only Justice Thomas dissenting, accepted the theory of a constructive discharge as a tangible employment action, but it also set conditions under which the employer could assert an affirmative defense and avoid strict liability under Title VII of the 1964 Civil Rights Act.[70] The issue was key to determining the scope of employers' vicarious liability in "supervisory" sexual harassment cases alleging a hostile work environment.

In *Faragher* and *Ellerth*, the Court had sought to clarify the nature and scope of an employer's legal liability for the discriminatory and harassing conduct of its supervisors in Title VII cases. It held employers strictly liable for a sexually hostile work environment created by a supervisor, when the challenged discrimination or harassment results in a "tangible employment action."[71] But in the absence of such a "company act" the employer may raise an affirmative defense based on its having in place a reasonable remedial process and on the employee's failure to take advantage of it. Thus, the *Ellerth/Faragher* defense has two components: "(a) that the employer exercised reasonable care to prevent and correct promptly any sexually harassing behavior, and (b) that the plaintiff employee unreasonably failed to take advantage of any preventative or corrective opportunities provided by the employer or to avoid harm otherwise."[72]

The Supreme Court defined a "tangible employment action" categorically to mean any "significant change in employment status," that may—but not always—result in economic harm. Specifically, the term includes "hiring, firing, failing to promote, reassignment with significantly different responsibilities, or a decision causing a significant change in benefits"[73] However, a "constructive discharge," where the employee quits, claiming that conditions are so intolerable that he or she was effectively "fired," presented an unresolved issue. Could an employer, faced with a claim of constructive discharge, still assert the *Ellerth/Faragher* defense?

Ultimately, the Court held that Title VII encompasses employer liability for constructive discharge claims attributable to a supervisor, but ruled that an "employer does not have recourse to the *Ellerth/Faragher* affirmative defense when a supervisor's official act precipitates the constructive discharge; absent such a 'tangible employment action,' however, the defense is available to the employer whose supervisors are charged with harassment."[74] In recognizing hostile environment constructive discharge claims, *Suders* enhanced Title VII protection for employees who quit their jobs over intense sexual harassment by a supervisor. But the decision also makes it easier for an employer to defend against such claims by showing that it has reasonable procedures for reporting and correcting harassment of which the employee failed to avail herself. Only "if the plaintiff quits in reasonable response to an employer-sanctioned adverse action officially changing her employment status or situation, for example, a humiliating demotion, extreme cut in pay, or transfer to a position in which she would face unbearable working condition," is the employer made strictly liable for monetary damages or other Title VII relief.[75]

Moreover, even where there has been a tangible employment action, coupled with a constructive discharge or resignation, the employer may have defenses available. First, the employer may argue that the harassing conduct did not occur as alleged, or was not sufficiently severe, pervasive, or unwelcome to meet standards for a Title VII violation. Second, if the tangible employment action is shown to be unrelated to the alleged harassment, or is taken for legitimate non-discriminatory reasons—particularly, if by persons other than the alleged harasser—the employer might escape liability. Finally, the employer might be able to demonstrate that, whatever form the underlying supervisory harassment may take, it did not meet the standard for constructive discharge: "so intolerable that a reasonable person would have felt compelled to resign."[76] But *Suders* also makes it more difficult to obtain summary judgment and avoid jury trials in sexual harassment cases involving constructive discharge claims. Under the decision, if there is any real dispute about whether the employee suffered a tangible employment action, the employer may not rely on the affirmative defense to obtain summary judgment.

Retaliation

In recent years, the Court has issued several decisions that have expanded the protections available under Title VII's anti-retaliation provision. In 2006, the Court issued its decision in *Burlington Northern & Santa Fe Railway Co. v. White*,[77] a case that involved questions about the scope of the retaliation provision under Title VII. In a 9-0 decision with one justice concurring, the Court held that the statute's retaliation provision encompasses any employer action that "would have been materially adverse to a reasonable employee or job applicant."[78] This standard, which is much broader than a standard that would have confined the retaliation provision to actions that affect only the terms and conditions of employment, generally makes it easier to sue employers if they retaliate against workers who complain about discrimination. Under the Court's interpretation, employees must establish only that the employer's actions might dissuade a worker from making a charge of discrimination. This means that an employee may successfully sue an employer for retaliation even if the employer's action does not actually result in an adverse employment action, such as being fired or losing wages.

In 2009, the Court issued a decision in *Crawford v. Metropolitan Government of Nashville and Davidson County*,[79] a case in which the plaintiff alleged that her participation in a sexual harassment investigation against her supervisor resulted in her termination. Although the plaintiff cooperated in the investigation and provided testimony regarding explicit comments and actions made by her boss, the fact that she had not filed the sexual harassment complaint or other charges with the Equal Employment Opportunity Commission (EEOC) led the lower court to rule that she was not covered under Title VII's retaliation provision. In reversing the decision, the

Court held that Title VII's retaliation provision encompasses retaliation against "an employee who speaks out about discrimination not on her own initiative, but in answering questions during an employer's internal investigation."[80] The Court emphasized that this result would prevent employers from undermining the purpose of Title VII by silencing employees who might fear being penalized if they reported discrimination during the course of an investigation.

More recently, the Court ruled in *Thompson v. North American Stainless*,[81] a sex discrimination case involving the question of whether Title VII creates a cause of action for third-party retaliation for individuals who have not personally engaged in protected activity. In *Thompson*, the plaintiff, who was fired three weeks after his then-fiancée filed a discrimination claim with the EEOC, alleged that his termination constituted unlawful retaliation in violation of Title VII, while the employer claimed that his discharge was for reasons of performance. The en banc Sixth Circuit, in a fractured opinion, held that the employee was not protected because he had not opposed any practice nor participated in a proceeding as required by the anti-retaliation provision of Title VII.[82]

In a unanimous decision, the Court reversed, holding that it had "little difficulty" in concluding that the "firing of Thompson violated Title VII."[83] Citing *Burlington*'s holding that Title VII's anti-retaliation provision prohibits actions that might dissuade a reasonable worker from complaining of discrimination, the Court declared "it obvious that a reasonable worker might be dissuaded from engaging in protected activity if she knew that her fiance would be fired."[84] The Court declined to establish fixed rules regarding the types of third-party relationships that are protected, but did indicate "that firing a close family member will almost always meet the *Burlington* standard, and inflicting a milder reprisal on a mere acquaintance will almost never do so...."[85]

Class Action Status

In *Wal-Mart v. Dukes*, the Supreme Court considered whether it was appropriate to approve class action status for up to 1.5 million current and former female employees of Wal-Mart retail stores nationwide. Alleging a pattern of sex discrimination, the plaintiffs claim that women were paid less than male workers in comparable positions and that the company systematically passed over female employees when awarding promotions to management. A federal district court certified the class.[86] Wal-Mart appealed the district court's class action certification, and a three-judge panel of the appellate court upheld the class action certification,[87] as did a subsequent ruling by a divided panel of appellate judges sitting en banc.[88] In a 5-4 decision, however, the Supreme Court reversed the class certification ruling.[89]

Under the Federal Rules of Civil Procedure, parties seeking class certification must show, among other things, that "(1) the class is so numerous that joinder of all members is impracticable, (2) there are questions of law or fact common to the class, (3) the claims or defenses of the representative parties are typical of the claims or defenses of the class, and (4) the representative parties will fairly and adequately protect the interests of the class."[90]

According to the Court, the *Wal-Mart* plaintiffs failed to meet the commonality requirement because they could not establish that Wal-Mart operated under a common, general policy of discrimination. Rather: "The only corporate policy that the plaintiffs' evidence convincingly establishes is Wal-Mart's 'policy' of allowing discretion by local supervisors over employment matters. On its face, of course, that is just the opposite of a uniform employment practice that would provide the commonality needed for a class action."[91]

In its ruling, the Court emphasized that plaintiffs must provide "significant proof" that a "specific employment practice" led to the discrimination, and rejected as insufficient statistical and anecdotal evidence offered by the plaintiffs.[92] Although the Court's decision makes it more difficult for employees to receive class certification and thus makes it less likely that large employers will face similar suits in the future, it is not the end of the litigation against Wal-Mart. The plaintiffs may still pursue their claims as individuals, or perhaps as part of a smaller class. Indeed, some of the Wal-Mart plaintiffs have reportedly filed a new lawsuit against the company but have limited their claims to the California stores.[93]

TITLE IX OF THE EDUCATION AMENDMENTS OF 1972

Title IX of the Education Amendments of 1972 prohibits discrimination on the basis of sex in educational programs and activities that receive federal funding. Until recently, Title IX claims have been most common among women and girls challenging inequities in sports programs,[94] but Title IX also provides a basis for challenging sexual harassment in classrooms and on campuses.

Title IX provides, in relevant part, that "[n]o person in the United States shall, on the basis of sex, be excluded from participation in, be denied the benefits of, or be subjected to discrimination under any education program or activity receiving Federal financial assistance.... "[95] The Court's recent decisions involving Title IX address various issues, including the availability of damages, the parties that are subject to liability, the scope of retaliation claims, and the availability of other statutory remedies.

In an early Title IX case, the Supreme Court held that the statute provides student victims with an avenue of judicial relief. In *Cannon v. University of Chicago*,[96] the Court ruled that an implied right of action exists under Title IX for student victims of sex discrimination who need not exhaust their administrative remedies before filing suit. However, the availability of monetary damages under Title IX remained uncertain until *Franklin v. Gwinnett County Public Schools*.[97] In *Franklin*, a female high school student brought an action for damages under Title IX against her school district alleging that she had been subjected to sexual harassment and abuse by a teacher. Although the harassment became known and an investigation was conducted, teachers and administrators did not act and the petitioner was subsequently discouraged from pressing charges. The Court, which found that sexual harassment by a teacher constituted discrimination on the basis of sex, held that damages were available to the sexual harassment victim if she could prove that the school district had intentionally violated Title IX.

After *Franklin*, it was clear that sexual harassment by a teacher constituted sex discrimination, but the extent to which school districts could be held liable for misconduct by its employees was less clear. The appropriate standard for measuring a school district's liability for sexual abuse of a student by a teacher remained unsettled until the Supreme Court ruling in *Gebser v. Lago Vista Independent School District*.[98] In *Gebser*, the Court determined that a school district will not be held liable under Title IX for a teacher's sexual harassment of a student if the school district did not have actual notice of the harassment and did not exhibit deliberate indifference to the misconduct.[99] The petitioner, a female high school student, was involved in a sexual relationship with one of her teachers. Unlike the situation in *Franklin*, the school district did not have actual notice of any sexual relationship between the petitioner and the teacher until they were discovered by a police officer. The principal of the petitioner's school did learn of inappropriate comments made by the teacher prior to the discovery, but he cautioned the teacher about such comments. After the sexual relationship became known, the school district quickly terminated the teacher. Despite the school district's actions, the petitioner argued that the school district should be found liable on the basis of vicarious liability or constructive notice.[100]

In requiring the school district to have actual notice of the harassment, the Court discussed the absence of an express cause of action under Title IX. Unlike Title VII, Title IX does not address damages or the particular situations in which damages are available.[101] While Title IX does address a denial of funds for noncompliance with its provisions, it does not provide for a private right of action. Instead, a private right of action has been judicially implied.[102]

Because Title IX does not contain any reference to the recovery of damages in private actions, the Court reasoned that its recognition of theories of vicarious liability and constructive notice would allow an unlimited recovery where Congress has not spoken.[103] Stated differently, the Court was reluctant to expand the availability of damages for such theories when Title IX failed to provide initially for a private cause of action. In this way, the Court sought to refine its holding in *Franklin* and limit those situations in which a remedy for damages would lie.

The Court believed that Title IX's remedial scheme would be undermined if it did not require that a school district have actual notice of a teacher's sexual harassment. Under Title IX, financial assistance will not be denied until the "appropriate person or persons" have been advised of the discrimination and have failed to end the discrimination voluntarily.[104] An "appropriate person" is an official of the entity receiving funds who has the authority to take corrective action.[105] Because the school district in *Gebser* did not have actual notice of the sexual relationship, it could not have taken any steps to end the alleged discrimination.

In addition, the Court stated that damages will not be available unless it is shown that a response exhibits a deliberate indifference to the discrimination; that is, there must be "an official decision by the recipient not to remedy the violation."[106] In *Gebser*, the school district responded to the situation by first cautioning the teacher, and then terminating him once the relationship was discovered. Thus, the Court concluded that the school district did not act with deliberate indifference.

Davis v. Monroe County Board of Education, decided in 1999, addressed the standard of liability that should be imposed on school districts to remedy student-on-student harassment.[107] The plaintiff in *Davis* alleged that her fifth-grade daughter had been harassed by another student over a prolonged period—a fact reported to teachers on several occasions—but that school officials had failed to take corrective action. Justice O'Connor, writing for a sharply divided Court, determined that the plaintiff had stated a Title IX claim. Because the statute restricts the actions of federal grant recipients, however, and not the conduct of third parties, the Court again refused to impose vicarious liability on the school district. Instead, "a recipient of federal funds may be liable in damages under Title IX only for its own misconduct."[108] School authorities' own "deliberate indifference" to student-on-student harassment could violate Title IX in certain cases. Thus, the Court held, where officials have "actual knowledge" of the harassment, where the "harasser is under the school's disciplinary authority," and where the harassment is so severe "that it can be said to deprive the victims of access to the educational opportunities or benefits provided by the school," the district may be held liable for damages under Title IX.[109]

While the development of sex discrimination law under Title IX owes much to Title VII, the *Davis* Court's recognition of student-on-student harassment highlights dramatic differences between the two statutes. Indeed, in qualifying the *Davis* standard, the Court suggested that student harassment may be far more difficult to prove than sexual harassment in employment. Beyond requiring "actual knowledge," Justice O'Connor cautioned that "schools are unlike adult workplaces" and disciplinary decisions of school administrators are not to be "second guess[ed]" by lower courts unless "clearly unreasonable" under the circumstances. Additionally, the majority emphasized that "[d]amages are not available for simple acts of teasing and name-calling among school children, even where these comments target differences in gender."[110] In effect, *Davis* left to school administrators the task of drawing the line between innocent teasing and actionable sexual harassment—a difficult and legally perilous task at best.

In a separate decision the same year, the Court found that a private organization is not subject to Title IX simply because it receives payments from entities that receive federal financial assistance. In *National Collegiate Athletic Association v. Smith*,[111] the respondent, a female graduate student, alleged that the National Collegiate Athletic Association (NCAA) discriminated against her on the basis of sex by denying her permission to play intercollegiate volleyball at two federally assisted institutions. Under NCAA rules, a graduate student is permitted to participate in intercollegiate athletics only at the institution that awarded her undergraduate degree. The respondent, who was enrolled at two different universities for her graduate degree, argued that the NCAA granted more waivers from eligibility restrictions to male graduate students than to female graduate students.

The Court concluded that the NCAA was not a recipient of Title IX funds because the NCAA did not receive federal assistance either directly or through an intermediary. Instead, it received dues payments from member institutions. The Court stated, "[a]t most, the Association's receipt of dues demonstrates that it indirectly benefits from the federal assistance afforded its members. This showing, without more, is insufficient to trigger Title IX coverage."[112] Because the Court found that the NCAA was not amenable to suit, it did not address the respondent's substantive allegations of discrimination.

In 2005, the Court handed down its decision in *Jackson v. Birmingham Board of Education*,[113] a case that further broadened the scope of Title IX to include protection against retaliation. In this case, which involved a girl's basketball coach who claimed that he was removed from his coaching position in retaliation for his complaints about unequal treatment of the girl's team, the Court held that Title IX not only encompasses retaliation claims, but also is available to individuals who complain about sex discrimination, even if such individuals themselves are not the direct victims of sex discrimination.[114] Reasoning that "Title IX's enforcement scheme would unravel" "if retaliation were not prohibited,"[115] the Court concluded that "when a funding recipient retaliates against a person because he complains of sex discrimination, this constitutes intentional discrimination on the basis of sex in violation of Title IX."[116]

More recently, the Court issued a decision in *Fitzgerald v. Barnstable School Committee*,[117] a case in which the Court considered whether Title IX provides the exclusive statutory remedy for unlawful sex discrimination in the education context. The lower court, concluding that Title IX was the exclusive statutory remedy, had rejected a claim that the original plaintiffs filed under 42 U.S.C. §1983 for violations of Title IX and the Equal Protection Clause of the Constitution.[118] In a unanimous decision, the Court reversed, holding that "Title IX was not meant to be an exclusive mechanism for addressing gender discrimination in schools, or a substitute for § 1983 suits as a means of enforcing constitutional rights."[119] As a result, plaintiffs may file claims related to sex discrimination in education under both statutes in the future.

End Notes

[1] U.S. Const. amend. XIV, §1; U.S. Const. amend. V.

[2] 42 U.S.C. §§2000e et seq.

[3] 20 U.S.C. §§1681 et seq.

[4] U.S. Const. amend. XIV, §1 (emphasis added).

[5] Tigner v. Texas, 310 U.S. 141, 147 (1940).

[6] *See* Ferguson v. Skrupa, 372 U.S. 726, 732 (1963).

[7] *See* San Antonio Indep. Sch. Dist. v. Rodriguez, 411 U.S. 1 (1973).

[8] *See* Craig v. Boren, 429 U.S. 190, 197 (1976). In *U.S. v. Virginia*, the Court required the Commonwealth of Virginia to provide an "exceedingly persuasive justification" for its policy of maintaining an all-male military academy. 518 U.S. 515 (1996). It is unclear whether this standard differs from the intermediate scrutiny standard of review. *See infra* text accompanying notes 16-34.

[9] *See* Lindsley v. Nat'l Carbonic Gas Co., 220 U.S. 61 (1911); Royster Guano Co. v. Virginia, 253 U.S. 412 (1920); San Antonio Indep. Sch. Dist. v. Rodriguez, 411 U.S. 1 (1973); Mass. Bd. of Ret. v. Murgia, 427 U.S. 307 (1976); Maher v. Roe, 432 U.S. 464 (1977).

[10] 429 U.S. 190 (1976).

[11] *Id.* at 198.

[12] *See, e.g.*, Califano v. Goldfarb, 430 U.S. 199 (1977) (invalidating section of the Social Security Act that permitted survivors' benefits for widowers only if they were receiving half of their support from their wives); Orr v. Orr, 440 U.S. 268 (1979) (invalidating Alabama statute that imposed alimony obligations on husbands, but not wives); Caban v. Mohammed, 441 U.S. 380 (1979) (invalidating New York statute that required the consent of the mother, but not the father, to permit the adoption of an illegitimate child); Mississippi University for Women v. Hogan, 458 U.S. 718 (1982) (invalidating policy of a state-supported university that limited admission to its nursing school to women on the grounds that it reinforced traditional stereotypes).

[13] 511 U.S. 127, 129 (1994).

[14] *Id.* at 132.

[15] *Id.* at 140.

[16] 518 U.S. 515 (1996).

[17] *Id.*

[18] *Id.* at 540.

[19] *Id.* at 533.

[20] *Id.* at 549.

[21] 523 U.S. 420 (1998).

[22] 8 U.S.C. §1409.

[23] Miller, 523 U.S. at 441.

[24] *Id.* at 443.

[25] 533 U.S. 53 (2001).

[26] *Id.* at 62.

[27] *Id.* at 63.

[28] *Id.*

[29] *Id.* at 65.

[30] *Id.* at 68-69.

[31] *Id.* at 70.

[32] *Id.* at 68.

[33] *Id.*

[34] *See, e.g., id.* at 70 ("We have explained that an 'exceedingly persuasive justification' is established 'by showing at least that the classification serves 'important governmental objectives and that the discriminatory means employed' are 'substantially related to the achievement of those objectives.' "); *id.* at 74 ("Because the Immigration and Naturalization Service (INS) has not shown an exceedingly persuasive justification for the sex based

classification embodied in 8 U.S.C. § 1409(a)(4)—i.e., because it has failed to establish at least that the classification substantially relates to the achievement of important governmental objectives—I would reverse the judgment of the Court of Appeals.").

[35] Title VII provides, in relevant part, that it is an unlawful employment practice for an employer "to fail or refuse to hire or to discharge any individual, or otherwise to discriminate against any individual with respect to his compensation, terms, conditions, or privileges of employment, because of such individual's race, color, religion, sex, or national origin; or to limit, segregate, or classify his employees or applicants for employment in any way which would deprive or tend to deprive any individual of employment opportunities or otherwise adversely affect his status as an employee, because of such individual's race, color, religion, sex, or national origin." 42 U.S.C. §2000e-2.

[36] 42 U.S.C. §2000e-2(e)(1).

[37] *See* Griggs v. Duke Power Co., 401 U.S. 424 (1971).

[38] A prima facie case is a case that contains elements that are sufficient to establish a claim unless disproved.

[39] *See*, McDonnell Douglas Corp. v. Green, 411 U.S. 792 (1973).

[40] 499 U.S. 187 (1991).

[41] *Id.* at 192.

[42] 42 U.S.C. §2000e(k).

[43] Johnson Controls, 499 U.S. at 202.

[44] *See, e.g.*, Dothard v. Rawlinson, 433 U.S. 321 (1977) (finding sex to be a BFOQ because the employment of a female guard in a maximum-security male penitentiary could create a risk of violence and jeopardize the safety of inmates); Western Airlines, Inc. v. Criswell, 472 U.S. 400 (1985) (finding age to be a BFOQ in an ADEA case because the employment of an older flight engineer could cause a safety emergency and jeopardize the safety of passengers).

[45] 129 S. Ct. 1962 (2009).

[46] *Id.* at 1968.

[47] 42 U.S.C. §2000e-2(h).

[48] 490 U.S. 228 (1989).

[49] *Id.* at 234-35.

[50] *Id.* at 250-51.

[51] Civil Rights Act of 1991, P.L. 102-166, §107(a).

[52] 42 U.S.C. §2000e-2(m).

[53] *Id.* at §2000e-5(g)(2).

[54] 539 U.S. 90 (2003).

[55] 477 U.S. 57 (1986).

[56] 510 U.S. 17 (1993).

[57] *Id.* at 22.

[58] *Id.* at 23.

[59] 42 U.S.C. §2000e-2.

[60] 523 U.S. 75, 77 (1998).

[61] *Id.* at 79.

[62] *Id.* at 80.

[63] 524 U.S. 775 (1998).

[64] *Id.* at 803.

[65] *Id.* at 805.

[66] 524 U.S. 742 (1998).

[67] *Id.* at 748.

[68] 527 U.S. 526 (1999).

[69] 542 U.S. 129 (2004).

[70] 42 U.S.C. §§2000e et seq.

[71] 524 U.S. 742, 765 (1998); 524 U.S. 775, 807 (1998).

[72] Suders, 542 U.S. at 137-38.

[73] Ellerth, 524 U.S. at 761.

[74] Suders, 542 U.S. at 140-141.

[75] *Id.* at 209.

[76] *Id.* at 147.

[77] 548 U.S. 53 (2006).

[78] *Id.* at 57.

[79] 129 S. Ct. 846 (2009).

[80] *Id.* at 849.

[81] 131 S. Ct. 863.

[82] 567 F.3d 804, 816 (6th Cir. 2009).

[83] Thompson v. N. Am. Stainless, LP, 131 S. Ct. 863, 867 (2011). The Court also held that Thompson is an aggrieved person within the meaning of Title VII and therefore has standing to sue. *Id.* at 869-70.

[84] *Id.* at 868.

[85] *Id.*

[86] Dukes et al. v. Wal-Mart Stores, Inc., 222 F.R.D. 137 (N.D.Cal. 2004).

[87] Dukes v. Wal-Mart, 509 F.3d 1168 (9th Cir. 2007).

[88] Dukes v. Wal-Mart Stores, Inc., 603 F.3d 571 (9th Cir. 2010).

[89] 131 S. Ct. 2541 (2011). The Court also unanimously held that claims for monetary relief may not be certified pursuant to Rule 23(b)(2), unless the monetary relief is incidental to the injunctive or declaratory relief. *Id.* at 2557.

[90] Fed. R. Civ. P. 23(a).

[91] Wal-Mart, 131 S. Ct. at 2554.

[92] *Id.* at 2553-56.

[93] Andrew Martin, "Female Wal-Mart Employees File New Bias Case," *New York Times*, October 27, 2011.

[94] See CRS Report RL31709, *Title IX, Sex Discrimination, and Intercollegiate Athletics: A Legal Overview*, by Jody Feder.

[95] 20 U.S.C. §1681(a).

[96] 441 U.S. 677 (1979).

[97] 503 U.S. 60 (1992).

[98] 524 U.S. 274 (1998).

[99] *Id.*

[100] Under a theory of constructive notice, liability would be established on the grounds that the school district knew or should have known about the harassment, but failed to discover and eliminate it.

[101] Gebser, 24 U.S. at 283-84.

[102] *See* Cannon v. University of Chicago, 441 U.S. 677 (1979). A private right of action allows an individual to sue in court for violations under a statute rather than wait for a federal agency to pursue a complaint administratively.

[103] Gebser, 524 U.S. at 286.

[104] 20 U.S.C. §1682.

[105] Gebser, 524 U.S. at 290.

[106] *Id.*

[107] 526 U.S. 629 (1999).

[108] *Id.* at 640.

[109] *Id.* at 650.

[110] *Id.* at 648-52.

[111] 525 U.S. 459 (1999).

[112] *Id.* at 468.

[113] 544 U.S. 167 (2005).

[114] *Id.* at 171.

[115] *Id.* at 180.

[116] *Id.* at 174 (internal quotations omitted).

[117] 129 S. Ct. 788 (2009).

[118] 42 U.S.C. §1983, which provides a remedy for deprivation of rights under color of state law, creates no new substantive rights but rather provides relief where state law is inadequate. Thus, individuals who sue under §1983 must find a source of rights elsewhere. As a result, §1983 is often used to enforce constitutional rights, such as the right to equal protection.

[119] Fitzgerald, 129 S. Ct. at 797.

In: Sex Discrimination and Harassment　　　ISBN 978-1-62257-466-7
Editors: H. Andrews and S. Spencer　　© 2012 Nova Science Publishers, Inc.

Chapter 3

Sexual Orientation and Gender Identity Discrimination in Employment: A Legal Analysis of the Employment Non-Discrimination Act (ENDA)[*]

Jody Feder and Cynthia Brougher

Summary

Introduced in various incarnations in every congressional session since the 103rd Congress, the proposed Employment Non-Discrimination Act (ENDA; H.R. 1397/S. 811) would prohibit discrimination based on an individual's actual or perceived sexual orientation or gender identity by public and private employers in hiring, discharge, compensation, and other terms and conditions of employment. The stated purpose of the legislation is "to address the history and widespread pattern of discrimination on the basis of sexual orientation or gender identity by private sector employers and local, State, and Federal Government employers," as well as to provide effective remedies for such discrimination. Patterned on Title VII of the Civil Rights Act of 1964, the act would be enforced by the Equal Employment Opportunity Commission (EEOC).

---

[*] This is an edited, reformatted and augmented version of Congressional Research Service, Publication No. R40934, dated May 23, 2011.

INTRODUCTION

Introduced in various incarnations in every congressional session since the 103rd Congress, the proposed Employment Non-Discrimination Act (ENDA; H.R. 1397/S. 811) would prohibit discrimination based on an individual's actual or perceived sexual orientation or gender identity by public and private employers in hiring, discharge, compensation, and other terms and conditions of employment. The stated purpose of the legislation is "to address the history and widespread pattern of discrimination on the basis of sexual orientation or gender identity by private sector employers and local, State, and Federal Government employers," as well as to provide effective remedies for such discrimination.[1] Specific exemptions from coverage are included for religious organizations and educational institutions, the armed services, and employers with fewer than 15 employees. Preferential treatment or quotas on the basis of sexual orientation or gender identity and "disparate impact" claims of discrimination would be specifically precluded. Patterned on Title VII of the Civil Rights Act of 1964,[2] the act would be enforced by the Equal Employment Opportunity Commission (EEOC).

Although earlier versions of the legislation, dating back to 1975, proposed simply amending the provisions of Title VII to add "sexual orientation" to categories of discrimination already prohibited, more recent versions of ENDA have proposed a stand-alone legislative safeguard against sexual orientation and gender identity discrimination in employment. Because the proposed legislation incorporates by reference many of Title VII's provisions, it is similar in scope to the earlier law. However, because discrimination on the basis of sexual orientation and gender identity was not before Congress when it enacted Title VII, the measures also differ in several significant respects.

COVERAGE

Like Title VII, ENDA would prohibit employers, employment agencies, and labor organizations from discriminating on the basis of sexual orientation or gender identity. Both public and private employers would be covered, although private employers who have fewer than 15 employees would be exempt. Like Title VII, ENDA would define "employer" to exclude "bona fide private membership" clubs that qualify for federal tax exemptions. As described in greater detail below, religious organizations and the Armed

Forces would also be specifically excluded from coverage under the legislation.

Likewise, most public and private employees would be protected by ENDA, including employees covered by the Government Employee Rights Act of 1991 and the Congressional Accountability Act of 1995.[3] Volunteers who receive no compensation, however, would not be covered under the legislation.

PROHIBITED ACTS

If enacted, ENDA would make it an unlawful employment practice for an employer to discriminate against an individual "because of an individual's actual or perceived sexual orientation or gender identity."[4] The legislation's delineation of prohibited employment practices substantially tracks the catalogue of employer malfeasance condemned by Title VII, which generally makes it unlawful for employers with 15 or more employees, employment agencies, and labor organizations to discriminate against employees or applicants for employment because of race, color, religion, sex, or national origin.[5] Thus, all forms of employment and preemployment bias would be forbidden, including discrimination in hiring, discharge, promotion, layoff and recall, compensation and fringe benefits, classification, training, apprentice-ship, referral, union membership, and other "terms, conditions, or privileges of employment." Likewise, employers would not be allowed to "limit, segregate, or classify" employees in ways that "deprive or tend to deprive" them of job opportunities or "adversely affect" their employment status. A comparable range of employment agency and labor organization practices, again largely borrowed from Title VII, would be prohibited by ENDA, which also would prohibit discrimination in apprenticeship or training programs. In addition, the legislation incorporates Title VII language that would specifically prohibit retaliation against employees who complain of discriminatory conduct.

Despite these similarities with respect to prohibited acts, ENDA would differ from Title VII in several significant ways. For example, one provision without direct parallel in Title VII's statutory text would make an employer liable for employment actions that are "based on the sexual orientation or gender identity of a person with whom the individual associates or has associated."[6] Another provision would narrow the evidentiary options available in sexual orientation and gender identity cases by stipulating that employees may bring only disparate treatment claims, meaning that disparate impact claims would be prohibited. Disparate treatment generally occurs when an employer intentionally discriminates against an employee by treating a similarly situated employee differently, while disparate impact occurs when an employer's acts or policies are facially neutral but have an adverse effect on a class of employees and are not otherwise reasonable. Proof of intent to discriminate is required to prove a disparate treatment claim, but is not required to establish a disparate impact claim, which can often be proved through the use of statistics. Because disparate impact claims would not be allowed under ENDA, a plaintiff would have to prove that an employer intended to discriminate, a higher evidentiary threshold. Reinforcing this limitation is another provision that would bar the EEOC from collecting statistics or from requiring employers to collect statistics on sexual orientation and gender identity.

In addition to these provisions, the ENDA legislation would clarify that preferential treatment or quotas on the basis of sexual orientation or gender identity would not be required, nor would employers be required to extend domestic partnership benefits. Likewise, employers would not be prohibited from requiring employees to adhere to reasonable dress or grooming standards, as long as the employer permits employees who have undergone gender transition to comply with the same dress or grooming standards for the gender to which the employee has transitioned or is transitioning. In a similar vein, ENDA would clarify that denying an employee access to shared shower or dressing facilities is not an unlawful employment practice, as long as the employer provides an employee with reasonable access to adequate facilities that are not inconsistent with the employee's gender identity, nor is construction of new or additional facilities required. Finally, ENDA would preserve the right of employers to enforce workplace rules and policies, provided that they "are designed for, and uniformly applied to, all individuals regardless of actual or perceived sexual orientation or gender identity."

Sexual Orientation

As noted above, ENDA would prohibit employment discrimination on the basis of actual or perceived sexual orientation. "Sexual orientation" would be defined to mean "homosexuality, heterosexuality, or bisexuality."[7] In contrast, Title VII's prohibition against discrimination on the basis of sex has consistently been interpreted to exclude discrimination on the basis of sexual orientation. Although some have argued that sex discrimination encompasses sexual orientation discrimination, the courts have generally rejected that theory, reasoning that the prohibition against sex discrimination refers only to the traditional definition of biological sex.[8] Because Title VII does not protect against employment discrimination on the basis of sexual orientation, ENDA would significantly expand the scope of protection under current employment discrimination law.

It is important to note, however, that courts have held that the fact that a victim of discrimination is gay or bisexual does not preclude a claim under Title VII. For example, in some cases, courts have allowed Title VII claims to proceed when an individual who is gay can demonstrate that he or she was the victim of unlawful sex discrimination in the form of sexual harassment or gender identity stereotyping.

In the context of sexual harassment, recent court decisions have been guided by the Supreme Court's decision in *Oncale v. Sundowner Offshore Services.*[9] In that case, a male employee suffered physical abuse of a sexual nature, but his claims of sexual harassment were initially denied because the lower court held that same-sex sexual harassment is not actionable under Title VII. The Supreme Court reversed, holding that, in cases of alleged sexual harassment, the gender of the victim and harasser are not dispositive, but rather the critical question is whether the harassment occurred "because of sex."[10] The Court also recognized that an inference that harassment is "because of sex" is not obvious where the harasser and the victim are of the same sex, but provided three examples of how such an inference could be established: (1) if the harasser sexually desired the victim; (2) if the harasser was hostile to the presence of one sex in the workplace; or (3) if comparative data showed that the harasser targeted only members of one sex.[11]

Based upon the Supreme Court's opinion in *Price Waterhouse v. Hopkins,*[12] individuals who are gay may also prevail under Title VII when an employer discriminates based on the employee's failure to conform to sex stereotypes. In *Price Waterhouse*, a female employee was denied partnership in an accounting firm, despite the fact that she was regarded as a high performer.[13] Furthermore, partners in the firm had instructed her to act more femininely in order to be considered for a partnership in the future.[14] The Court held that Price Waterhouse was applying standards for partnership in a prohibited sexually disparate manner, in that Title VII did not permit an employer to evaluate female employees based upon their conformity with the employer's stereotypical view of femininity.[15] As a result, harassment of an individual for failure to conform to sex stereotypes could constitute harassment "because of sex," even if the animosity towards nonconformance is caused by a belief that such behavior indicates homosexuality.

Based on these decisions, it appears that individuals who are gay may currently be protected under Title VII if they are discriminated against because of sex. However, such individuals would not be protected by current law if they were the victim of discrimination on the basis of sexual orientation, a situation that ENDA appears designed to remedy. It is important to note that ENDA states that the act should not be construed to invalidate or limit rights under any other federal or state law. Therefore, ENDA would not appear to alter the current protections that may be available to individuals who are gay under Title VII or state law.

Gender Identity

ENDA would also prohibit employment discrimination on the basis of actual or perceived gender identity. "Gender identity" would be defined to mean "the gender-related identity, appearance, or mannerisms or other gender-related characteristics of an individual, with or without regard to the individual's designated sex at birth." Under current law, Title VII does not expressly prohibit gender identity discrimination. Nonetheless, there have been cases interpreting Title VII's prohibition against sex discrimination to cover gender and/or gender identity. Although the majority of federal courts to consider the issue have concluded that discrimination on the basis of gender identity is not sex discrimination,[16] there have been several courts that have reached the opposite conclusion in the years since the Supreme Court's decision in *Price Waterhouse*. As noted above, the *Price Waterhouse* decision, in which the Court repeatedly declared that Title VII bars discrimination on the basis of "gender," held that discrimination against a female employee who did not conform to socially constructed gender expectations constituted unlawful gender discrimination in violation of Title VII. Since *Price Waterhouse*, several courts have openly speculated that the *Price Waterhouse* decision "seem[s] to indicate that the word 'sex' in Title VII encompasses both gender and sex, and forbids discrimination because of one's failure to act in a way expected of a man or a woman."[17]

For example, in *Smith v. Salem*, a male firefighter who was undergoing gender transition to female argued that he had been suspended because of his feminine appearance.[18] The Sixth Circuit held that, to the extent that the firefighter asserted that she experienced discriminatory treatment due to the fact that she did not conform to what her employer believed males should look and act like, she had sufficiently plead a prima facie case of sex discrimination.[19] Similarly, in *Barnes v. Cincinnati*, a male police officer undergoing gender transition to female was denied a promotion because she acted too femininely in her supervisors' opinions.[20]

Although some courts have held that Title VII's prohibition against sex discrimination may encompass claims based on gender identity when unlawful gender stereotyping is involved, the courts have not recognized gender identity discrimination on its own to be an unlawful employment practice under Title VII. As a result, ENDA would significantly expand the scope of protection under current employment law by explicitly prohibiting gender identity discrimination. As noted above, ENDA states that the act should not be construed to invalidate or limit rights under any other federal or state law. Therefore, ENDA would not appear to alter the current protections based on gender identity that may be available under Title VII or state law.

EXCEPTIONS FOR THE ARMED FORCES AND RELIGIOUS ORGANIZATIONS

ENDA contains several exceptions. First, the Armed Forces, which include the Army, Navy, Air Force, Marines, and Coast Guard, would be exempt, and the legislation specifies that current laws regarding veterans' preferences in employment would not be affected. The courts have similarly held that uniformed military personnel are not covered by Title VII,[21] although civilian military employees are protected by Title VII.[22]

Notably, certain religious organizations would also be exempt from coverage under ENDA. This exemption is consistent with previous congressional efforts to avoid infringing on a religious organization's exercise of religion with respect to its employment practices, such as the Title VII provision that exempts certain religious organizations from compliance with that statute. In that sense, ENDA would expand the current protection offered to religious organizations relating to discrimination in employment practices.

Title VII includes two exceptions that allow certain employers to consider religion in employment decisions. Specifically, the prohibition against religious discrimination does not apply to "a religious corporation, association, educational institution, or society with respect to the employment of individuals of a particular religion to perform work connected with the carrying on by such corporation, association, educational institution, or society of its activities."[23] The prohibition also does not apply to religious educational institutions if the institution "is, in whole or in substantial part, owned, supported, controlled, or managed by a particular religion or by a particular [organization], or if the curriculum of the [institution] is directed toward the propagation of a particular religion."[24] These exemptions are sometimes referred to as sections 702(a) and 703(e)(2), respectively. The Title VII exemptions apply with respect to discrimination based on religion only and do not allow qualifying organizations to discriminate on any other basis forbidden by Title VII, such as race, color, national origin, or sex.[25]

Like Title VII, ENDA "shall not apply to a corporation, association, educational institution or institution of learning, or society that is exempt from the religious discrimination provisions of title VII of the Civil Rights Act of 1964 pursuant to section 702(a) or 703(e)(2) of such Act."[26] By exempting the organizations covered by the 702(a) and 703(e)(2) exemptions of Title VII, ENDA ensures that such organizations would not be required to hire or retain an individual if the organization had objections to the individual's sexual orientation or gender identity. Notably, the language of Title VII does not appear to require that the organization's religious beliefs oppose certain sexual orientations or gender identifications. In other words, the ENDA exemption does not appear to limit the permissibility of religious organizations' discrimination based on sexual orientation or gender identity to instances in which those factors may conflict with religious beliefs. For example, under the legislation, even religious organizations whose religious teachings do not oppose homosexuality could be permitted to refuse to hire a gay applicant. Thus, the proposed legislation likely would not interfere with religious organizations' employment practices involving considerations of sexual orientation or gender identity of employees and applicants. To the contrary, it may actually broaden these organizations' ability to discriminate in hiring. In this sense, the ENDA exception goes farther than the Title VII exception, which allows religious employers to discriminate on the basis of religion but not on the basis of race, color, national origin, or sex.

The question of what organizations would be covered by the ENDA exemption may be resolved by looking at organizations that have sought protection under the relevant Title VII exemptions. Title VII did not define what organizations would qualify for an exemption under the statute, and court decisions have indicated several factors relevant to deciding whether an organization qualifies, including (1) the purpose or mission of the organization; (2) the ownership, affiliation, or source of financial support of the organization; (3) requirements placed upon staff and members of the organization (faculty and students if the organization is a school); and (4) the extent of religious practices in or the religious nature of products and services offered by the organization.[27] No single factor appears to be dispositive and as one federal court has noted, "the decision whether an organization is 'religious' for purposes of the exemption cannot be based on its conformity to some preconceived notion of what a religious organization should do, but must be measured with reference to the particular religion identified by the organization."[28]

Organizations may qualify for an exemption if their purpose, character, and operations incorporate elements of their religion. For example, in *LeBoon v. Lancaster Jewish Community Center Association*, a Jewish community center qualified for an exemption under Title VII when it terminated the employment of a Christian employee.[29] The center's stated mission was to promote Jewish life and values, and three local rabbis were significantly involved in its management. Furthermore, the center conducted a variety of programs observing Jewish religious holidays and traditions. The Third Circuit noted the organization's primarily religious character, indicated by factors such as the composition of its administrative body and the programs that it offered to the community. Ultimately, the court held that religious organizations may qualify for an exemption despite engaging in secular activities, not adhering to the strictest tenets of the religion, or not hiring only co-religionists.[30]

On the other hand, courts have declined to apply the exemption to organizations that cannot demonstrate a connection between religious beliefs and the organization itself. In *Equal Employment Opportunity Commission (EEOC) v. Townley Engineering and Manufacturing Company*, the owners of a mining equipment manufacturing company claimed an exemption under Title VII after an employee initiated legal proceedings objecting to attending mandatory religious services.[31] The owners claimed that they founded their company under "a covenant with God that their business would be a Christian, faith-operated business" and that they were "unable to separate God from any portion of their daily lives, including their activities at the Townley company."[32] The court reviewed legal precedent and the legislative history of Title VII and held that the central function of the exemption "has been to exempt churches, synagogues, and the like, and organizations closely affiliated with those entities."[33] It noted that Townley was a for-profit company, producing a secular product, with no affiliation with or support from a church. Further, it had no religious purpose. Although the court recognized that the owners did include religious characteristics in their operation of their company, the court held that "the beliefs of the owners and operators of a corporation are not simply enough in themselves to make the corporation 'religious'" under the Title VII exemption.[34]

In *Pime v. Loyola University of Chicago*, a former Jesuit university sought to retain its religious identity even after it had evolved into a secular institution.[35] It claimed an exemption under Title VII as a university supported, controlled, or managed in whole or in part by a religious society because it reserved three tenured positions for Jesuits and several university administrators (including the president, one-third of the trustees, and other officers) were also Jesuits. However, the Society of Jesus did not instruct the president or trustees with regard to university matters and did not control the decisions of other Jesuits who served in official positions at the university.[36]

As a result, the Seventh Circuit held that, despite a "Jesuit presence" on campus, the university did not qualify for an exemption from Title VII.[37]

In a similar case, *EEOC v. Kamehameha Schools/Bishop Estate*, the Ninth Circuit likewise held that a school that hired Protestant teachers to provide a secular education to students did not qualify for an exemption under Title VII.[38] The Kamehameha Schools were created by the will of a member of the Hawaiian royal family, which provided that teachers be members of the Protestant faith and claimed an exemption as a religious educational institution based on this provision. However, the court held that the schools' purpose and character were primarily secular and not religious, noting that the religious characteristics the schools had (i.e., comparative religious studies, scheduled prayers and services, Bible quotations in a school publication, and employment of nominally Protestant teachers) were common to private schools. The court also noted that the schools had embraced a broad mandate to help native Hawaiians "participate in contemporary society for a rewarding and productive life" through a solid secular education.[39] As a result, the court held that the teachers' religious affiliation was an insufficient basis to qualify for an exemption as a religious institution.

The result in *Kamehameha Schools* was influenced to some degree by the absence of church ownership or control. Indeed, the court of appeals observed that it had found "no case holding the Title VII exemption to be applicable where the institution was not wholly or partially owned by a church."[40] Subsequently, in *Killinger v. Samford University*,[41] the Eleventh Circuit held that a Baptist college was an exempt religious institution which could require professors to subscribe to the school's religious doctrine. The court noted that a Baptist convention comprised the largest single source of revenue for the college and that the school's charter listed as its chief purpose the "promotion of Christian Religion." Thus, under Title VII precedent, independent Christian and other religious schools not owned, financed, or controlled by church bodies may find it difficult to qualify for the "religious organization" exemption in ENDA. Of course, as stand-alone legislation, it is possible that courts would find that the policy concerns underlying ENDA are sufficiently different from Title VII to warrant a less restrictive reading of the former. Absent clarification in ENDA itself, or its legislative history, any resolution of the issue would have to await further judicial elaboration.

ENFORCEMENT AND REMEDIES

Enforcement procedures under ENDA would parallel the enforcement provisions of Title VII. Thus, the Department of Justice (DOJ) would enforce ENDA against state and local governments, and administrative enforcement with respect to private employment would be delegated to the EEOC, which would have the same authority to receive and investigate complaints, to negotiate voluntary settlements, and to seek judicial remedies as it currently exercises under Title VII. Similarly, in devising remedies for sexual orientation or gender identity discrimination under the legislation, a federal court would have the same jurisdiction and powers as the court has to enforce Title VII. In general, federal courts possess broad remedial discretion under Title VII, including the ability to enjoin the unlawful employment practice and to "order such affirmative action as may be appropriate, which may include, but is not limited to, reinstatement or hiring of employees, with or without back pay ... or any other relief as the court deems appropriate."[42] Although the Supreme Court early on adopted a "make-whole" theory of Title VII relief,[43] including use of affirmative action remedies, minority preferences and the like, where necessary to redress discrimination of a particularly "egregious" or "longstanding" nature, ENDA would specifically forbid employers from using quotas or preferential treatment.

Likewise, the remedies under ENDA would be patterned on Title VII's remedial provisions. Under Title VII, victims of discrimination may seek equitable relief, including limited back pay awards for wage, salary, and fringe benefits lost as the result of discrimination. Private employers who intentionally discriminate in violation of the statute may be liable for compensatory and punitive damages, while plaintiffs may seek awards of compensatory, but not punitive, damages against federal, state, and local governmental agencies. The following ceilings or "caps" are established by law for compensatory and punitive damages combined: (1) $50,000 for defendants who have 15 to 100 employees; (2) $100,000 for employers with 101 to 200 employees; (3) $200,000 for employers with 201 to 500 employees; and (4) $300,000 for employers with more than 500 employees.[44] The Supreme Court has also excluded from the statutory limits on damages so-called "front pay," awarded to redress discrimination victims for continuing injury in promotion or discharge cases where reinstatement is not a feasible remedy.[45] These Title VII remedies appear to be applicable to claims that would be filed under ENDA.

Meanwhile, ENDA would waive the states' Eleventh Amendment immunity from suit for sexual orientation discrimination or gender identity against employees or applicants within any state "program or activity" that receives federal financial assistance. The Eleventh Amendment provides states with immunity from claims brought under federal law in both federal and state courts.[46] Although Congress may waive the states' sovereign immunity by "appropriate" legislation enacted pursuant to § 5 of the Fourteenth Amendment,[47] the scope of congressional power to create a private right of action against the states for monetary damages has been substantially narrowed by a series of Supreme Court decisions.

The era of a reinvigorated Eleventh Amendment immunity can be traced to *Seminole Tribe v. Florida*,[48] which invalidated a portion of the Indian Gaming Regulatory Act authorizing tribal suits against the states. Neither the Commerce Clause nor § 5 proved to be an effective vehicle to override state sovereign immunity. Three years later, in *Alden v. Maine*[49] the Supreme Court ruled that the states could not be sued, even in their own courts, for violation of the Fair Labor Standards Act. *City of Boerne v. Flores*[50] announced the Court's new framework for determining the validity of congressional action under § 5. In holding unconstitutional the Religious Freedom Restoration Act, Justice Kennedy wrote that Congress's § 5 power was remedial only; it was not a basis for legislation defining the substantive content of the equal protection guarantee. Moreover, the remedy had to be "congruent and proportional" to the scope and frequency of any violations identified by Congress. These constitutional limitations were subsequently applied by the Court to hold the states immune from private lawsuits under the Age Discrimination in Employment Act,[51] the Violence Against Women Act,[52] and the Americans with Disabilities Act.[53]

Taken together, these decisions restrict the ability of private individuals to take the states to court for federal civil rights violations. They may not, however, apply to states' voluntary acceptance of federal benefits that are expressly conditioned on waiver of Eleventh Amendment immunity. "Congress may, in the exercise of its spending power, condition its grant of funds to the States upon their taking certain actions that Congress could not require them to take, and that acceptance of the funds entails an agreement to the actions."[54] Thus, when a statute enacted under the Spending Clause[55] conditions grants to the states upon an unambiguous waiver of Eleventh Amendment immunity, as ENDA proposes, "the condition is constitutionally permissible as long as it rests on the state's voluntary and knowing acceptance of it."[56]

Finally, the attorney's fees provision in ENDA is substantially identical to Title VII, which states

> In any action or proceeding under this subchapter the court, in its discretion, may allow the prevailing party, other than the Commission or the United States, a reasonable attorney's fee (including expert fees) as part of the costs, and the Commission and the United States shall be liable for costs the same as a private person.[57]

Under Title VII, a "prevailing" plaintiff is ordinarily entitled to attorney's fees unless special circumstances make such an award unjust.[58] Complainants may be considered "prevailing parties" if "they succeed on any significant issue in litigation which achieves some of the benefit the parties sought in bringing the suit."[59] Although either a plaintiff or a defendant may be the prevailing party, fee awards to defendant employers are not the general rule, given the public interest in having Title VII plaintiffs act as "private attorneys general" and the likelihood that defendant employers would have less need of financial assistance.[60]

End Notes

[1] H.R. 1397/S. 811, § 2, 112th Cong.

[2] 42 U.S.C. §§ 2000e et seq.

[3] *Id.* at § 2000e-16; 2 U.S.C. § 1301.

[4] H.R. 1397/S. 811, § 4, 112th Cong.

[5] 42 U.S.C. § 2000e-2.

[6] It is important to note that the scope of legal protection afforded persons based on their "perceived" orientation may be difficult to gauge. There is no comparable language in Title VII prohibiting discrimination on the basis of "perceived" characteristics applicable to

discrimination prohibited by the statute. Thus, courts would apparently be left the task of developing appropriate standards of proof in such "perceived" orientation cases.

[7] The legislation does not define these terms, although the terms are defined elsewhere in the U.S. Code, in the context of the military. 10 U.S.C. § 654(f) (2007). Among the states that do prohibit discrimination on the basis of sexual orientation, it is almost universally defined as including homosexuality, bisexuality, or heterosexuality. *See* Government Accounting Office, *Sexual Orientation-Based Employment Discrimination: States' Experience with Statutory Prohibitions* at 2-4, tbl.1, July 9, 2002, available at http://www.gao.gov/new.items/d02878r.pdf.

[8] *See, e.g.,* Spearman v. Ford Motor Co., 231 F.3d 1080 (7th Cir. 2000); Higgins v. New Balance Ath. Shoe, Inc., 194 F.3d 252 (1st Cir. 1999); Williamson v. A.G. Edwards & Sons, Inc., 876 F.2d 69 (8th Cir. 1989); DeSantis v. Pacific Tel. and Tel. Co., 608 F.2d 327 (9th Cir. 1979); Smith v. Liberty Mut. Ins. Co., 569 F.2d 325 (5th Cir. 1978).

[9] 523 U.S. 75 (1998).

[10] *Id.* at 77, 81.

[11] *Id.* at 80-81.

[12] 490 U.S. 228 (1989).

[13] *Id.* at 233-234.

[14] *Id.* at 235.

[15] *Id.* at 250-251.

[16] *See, e.g.,* Ulane v. Eastern Airlines, 742 F.2d 1081 (7th Cir. 1984); Sommers v. Budget Mktg., Inc., 667 F.2d 748, 750 (8th Cir.1982); Holloway v. Arthur Andersen, 566 F.2d 659 (9th Cir. 1977); Etsitty v. Utah Transit Auth., 502 F.3d 1215 (10th Cir. 2007).

[17] Enriquez v. West Jersey Health Sys., 342 N.J. Super. 501, 512 (App. Div. 2001) (holding that a New Jersey state law barring sex discrimination in employment includes gender discrimination and thus protects transsexuals). *See also*, Smith v. City of Salem, 378 F.3d 566 (6th Cir. 2004); Schwenk v. Hartford, 204 F.3d 1187, 1201-02 (9th Cir. 2000); Schroer v. Billington, 424 F. Supp. 2d 203 (D.D.C. 2006).

[18] 378 F.3d 566 (6th Cir. 2004).

[19] *Id.* at 575.

[20] 401 F.3d 729 (6th Cir. 2005).

[21] *See, e.g.,* Luckett v. Bure, 290 F.3d 493 (2d Cir. 2002).

[22] 42 U.S.C. § 2000e-16(a).

[23] *Id.* at § 2000e-1(a).

[24] *Id.* at § 2000e-2(e)(2).

[25] *See* EEOC v. Pacific Press Publ'g Ass'n, 676 F.2d 1272, 1276 (9th Cir. 1982); EEOC Notice N-915, Sept. 23, 1987.

[26] H.R. 1397/S. 811, § 6, 112th Cong. (citations omitted).

[27] *See* LeBoon v. Lancaster Jewish Cmty. Ctr. Ass'n, 503 F.3d 217, 226-27 (3rd Cir. 2007) (providing a summary discussion of circuit courts' interpretations of organizations that qualify under Title VII's exemption).

[28] *Id.*

[29] *Id.*

[30] *Id.* at 229-230.

[31] 859 F.2d 610 (9th Cir. 1988).

[32] *Id.* at 611-12 (internal quotations omitted).

[33] *Id.* at 618.

[34] *Id.* at 619.

[35] 585 F. Supp. 435 (N.D. Ill. 1984), aff'd, 803 F.2d 351 (7th Cir. 1986).

[36] *Id.* at 440-41.

[37] *Id.*

[38] 990 F.2d 458 (9th Cir. 1993).

[39] *Id.* at 462-63 (internal quotations omitted).

[40] *Id.* at 461, n. 7.

[41] 113 F.3d 196 (11th Cir. 1997).

[42] 42 U.S.C. § 2000e-5(g).

[43] For more information, see CRS Report RL30470, *Affirmative Action in Employment: A Legal Overview*, by Jody Feder.

[44] 42 U.S.C. § 1981a(b).

[45] Pollard v. E.I. du Pont de Nemours & Co., 532 U.S. 843 (2001).

[46] U.S. Const. amend. XI.

[47] U.S. Const. amend. XIV.

[48] 517 U.S. 44 (1996).

[49] 527 U.S. 706 (1999).

[50] 521 U.S. 507 (1997).

[51] Kimel v. Bd. of Regents, 528 U.S. 62 (2000).

[52] United States v. Morrison, 529 U.S. 598 (2000).

[53] Bd. of Trs. of the Univ. of Ala. v. Garrett, 531 U.S. 356 (2001).

[54] College Savings Bank v. Florida Prepaid Postsecondary Educ. Expense Bd., 527 U.S. 666, 686 (1999).

[55] U.S. Const. art. I, § 8, cl. 1.

[56] Litman v. George Mason Univ., 186 F.3d 544, 555 (4th Cir. 1999). For more information on waiving state sovereign immunity, see CRS Report RL30315, *Federalism, State Sovereignty, and the Constitution: Basis and Limits of Congressional Power*, by Kenneth R. Thomas.

[57] 42 U.S.C. § 2000e-5(k).

[58] Albermarle Paper Co. v. Moody, 442 U.S. 405 (1975); New York Gaslight Club, Inc. v. Carey, 447 U.S. 54 (1980).

[59] Hensley v. Eckherhart, 461 U.S. 424 (1983).

[60] Christiansburg Garment Co. v. EEOC, 434 U.S. 412 (1978).

In: Sex Discrimination and Harassment   ISBN 978-1-62257-466-7
Editors: H. Andrews and S. Spencer   © 2012 Nova Science Publishers, Inc.

Chapter 4

PAY EQUITY LEGISLATION[*]

Benjamin Collins and Jody Feder

SUMMARY

The term "pay equity" originates from the fact that women as a group are paid less than men. In recent years, for example, women with a strong commitment to the workforce earned about 77 to 80 cents for every dollar earned by men. As women's earnings as a percentage of men's earnings have narrowed by less than 20 percentage points over the past 40-plus years, some members of the public policy community have argued that current anti-discrimination laws should be strengthened and that additional measures should be enacted. Others, in contrast, believe that further government intervention is unnecessary because the gender wage gap will narrow on its own as women's labor market qualifications continue to more closely resemble those of men.

The Equal Pay Act (EPA), which amends the Fair Labor Standards Act (FLSA), prohibits covered employers from paying lower wages to female employees than male employees for "equal work" on jobs requiring "equal skill, effort, and responsibility" and performed "under similar working conditions" at the same location. The FLSA exempts some jobs (e.g., hotel service workers) from EPA coverage, and the EPA makes exceptions for wage differentials based on merit or seniority systems, systems that measure earnings by "quality or quantity" of production, or "any factor other than sex." The "equal work" standard

---

[*] This is an edited, reformatted and augmented version of Congressional Research Service, Publication No. RL31867, dated June 1, 2012.

embodies a middle ground between demanding that two jobs either be exactly alike or that they merely be comparable. The test applied by the courts focuses on job similarity and whether, given all the circumstances, they require substantially the same skill, effort, and responsibility. The EPA may be enforced by the government, or individual complainants, in civil actions for wages unlawfully withheld and liquidated damages for willful violations. In addition, Title VII of the 1964 Civil Rights Act provides for the awarding of compensatory and punitive damages to victims of "intentional" wage discrimination, subject to caps on the employer's monetary liability.

The issue of pay equity has attracted substantial attention in recent Congresses. A number of measures, including bills that would provide additional remedies, mandate "equal pay for equivalent jobs," or require studies on pay inequity, have been introduced in each of the last several congressional sessions. These bills include the Paycheck Fairness Act (H.R. 1519/S. 3220) and the Fair Pay Act (H.R. 1493/S. 788). Meanwhile, in *Wal-Mart Stores v. Dukes*, the Supreme Court recently rejected class action status for current and former female Wal-Mart employees who allege that the company has engaged in pay discrimination.

The persistence of gender-based wage disparities—commonly referred to as the pay or wage gap—has been the subject of extensive debate and commentary. Congress first addressed the issue more than four decades ago in the Equal Pay Act of 1963,[1] mandating an "equal pay for equal work" standard, and addressed it again the following year in Title VII of the 1964 Civil Rights Act.[2] Collection of compensation data and elimination of male/female pay disparities are also integral to Labor Department enforcement of Executive Order 11246, which mandates nondiscrimination and affirmative action by federal contractors. During the 1980s, some members of the public policy community sought to advance the earnings of women relative to men by pressing a "comparable worth" theory before state legislatures and in federal court litigation. During the last several decades, initiatives to strengthen and expand current federal remedies available to victims of unlawful sex-based wage discrimination have been taken up in Congress.

This report begins by showing the trend in the male-female wage gap and by examining the explanations that have been offered for its enduring presence. It next discusses the major laws directed at eliminating sex-based

wage discrimination as well as relevant federal court cases. The report closes
with a description of pay equity legislation that has been considered or enacted
by Congress in recent years.

THE GENDER WAGE GAP

Historical and Current Trends

Disparities between the pay of male and female workers are well-
established, though the magnitude of the difference has decreased over time.
In 1960, the median earnings for females employed full-time, year-round (i.e.,
50-52 weeks per year and at least 35 hours per week) were 60.7% of males'
median earnings. By 2010, the median earnings for female workers employed
full-time year-round were 77.4% of the earnings of male workers with the
same level of labor force attachment.[3]

Figure 1 charts the ratio of median female earnings to median male
earnings since 1960. While there is a clear long-term narrowing of the wage
gap, the rate of change has varied. Between 1960 and 1980, the gap was fairly
consistent, with female earnings varying between 56.6% and 60.7% of male
earnings. Throughout the 1980s, the gap narrowed relatively quickly, and by
1990, female earnings were almost 72% of male earnings. Since then, the gap
has narrowed at a slower rate, and since 2004, female earnings have been
between 76.6% and 77.4% of male earnings.

Further examination of Census data from 2010 show that male-female
earnings disparities persist even after controlling for common predictors of
personal earnings. For example, the median earnings for female workers with
a bachelor's degree and employed full-time year-round were 72.4% of those of
male workers in the same category. Among full-time year-round workers in
professional and related occupations, the median earnings for female workers
were 73.1% of those of male workers.[4] Female workers also earn less than
male workers in the same age range, though the differences tend to be
narrower among younger workers. Among full-time year-round workers
between the ages of 15 and 24, females' earnings were 89.0% of males'.
Among workers age 45 to 64, female workers earned about 73.4% of what
males did. While some interpret these data as evidence of gender-based
discrimination, it is important to note that they do not account for all
characteristics that can legitimately affect earnings such as college major or
uninterrupted years of employment.

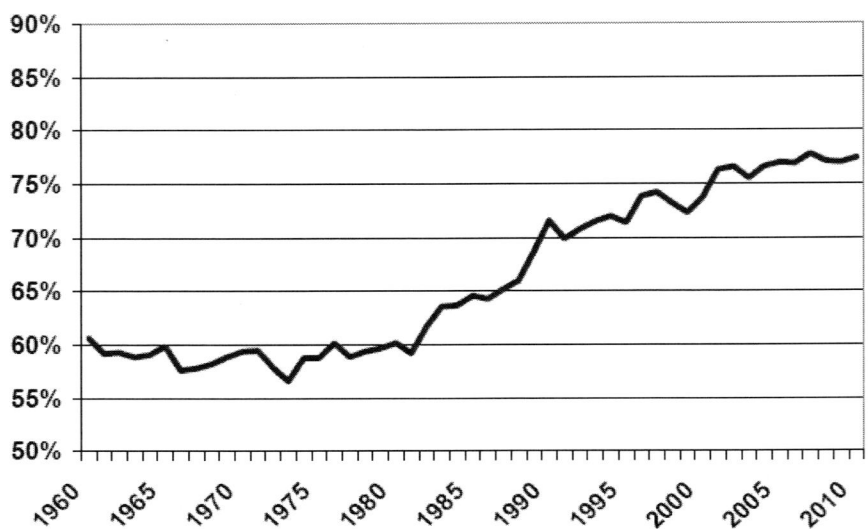

Source: Graph constructed by CRS using data from the United States Census Bureau, *Income, Poverty, and Health Insurance Coverage in the United States: 2010*, September 2011, Table A-5. Full report available at http://www.census.gov/prod/2011pubs/p60-239.pdf.

Note: Data include all workers age 15 and over.

Figure 1. Female Earnings as a Share of Male Earnings, 1960-2010; Median earnings, full-time year-round workers.

Explanations of and Remedies for the Gender Pay Differential

Two primary schools of thought have developed to explain the persistence of the wage gap. The human capital explanation has a supply-side focus—that is, it looks at the personal characteristics of working women and men. The occupational sex segregation explanation has a demand-side focus—that is, it looks at the characteristics of the jobs in which women and men typically work.

The human capital explanation posits that there are fundamental differences in the skill sets of male and female workers, and that these differences in human capital explain the wage gap. Proponents of this perspective suggest that as male and female workers' human capital characteristics continue to converge, the wage gap will be eliminated. They thus believe that no government intervention is warranted to achieve pay equity beyond current anti-discrimination measures.

The sex segregation explanation recognizes that men and women cluster in different occupations, and that the jobs in which women concentrate tend to have lower wages. Proponents of the sex segregation explanation suggest that jobs in which female workers cluster are paid relatively low wages not because they are less demanding than higher-paid jobs, but because they are predominantly held by women.

Supporters of the sex segregation explanation often support government action beyond enforcement of existing anti-discrimination laws. They support, for instance, increased dissemination of information and provision of training in high-paying jobs in which women are underrepresented.[5] Advocates have also suggested that pay within firms should be set by the "comparable worth" principle. Under this premise, jobs within a firm are evaluated and pay is set by skills, responsibilities, and working conditions. Comparable worth proponents suggest that setting pay in this way will raise the pay in female-dominated occupations and close the wage gap.[6]

The human capital explanation and occupational sex segregation explanations are not mutually exclusive. Indeed, some researchers have used a combination of the explanations to explain a considerable portion of the wage gap.[7] There is no widely accepted methodology, however, that explains the entirety of the wage gap, leaving ambiguity as to what role, if any, employer bias may play in the wage gap.

LEGAL AND LEGISLATIVE BACKGROUND

Laws That Combat Sex-Based Wage Discrimination

The Equal Pay Act (EPA) is a 1963 amendment to the Fair Labor Standards Act that makes it illegal to pay different wages to employees of the opposite sex for equal work on jobs the performance of which requires "equal skill, effort, and responsibility," and which are "performed under similar working conditions."[8] The act also prohibits labor organizations and their agents from causing or attempting to cause sex-based wage discrimination by employers. Specifically permitted by the EPA, however, are wage differentials based on seniority systems, merit systems, systems that measure earnings by quality or quantity of production, or "any factor other than sex."[9] The "equal work" standard embodies a middle ground between demanding that two jobs be either exactly alike or that they merely be comparable. The test applied by the courts focuses on job similarity and whether, in light of all the circumstances, they require substantially the same skill, effort, and responsibility.[10] An employer may not attempt to equalize wages to comply with the EPA by lowering the rate of pay for any employee.[11]

A year after passage of the EPA, Congress enacted the comprehensive code of anti-discrimination rules based on race, color, national origin, religion, and sex found in Title VII of the Civil Rights Act. The EPA and Title VII provide overlapping coverage for claims of sex-based wage discrimination, but differ in important substantive, procedural, and remedial aspects. A crucial difference is that the "equal work" standard of the EPA—requiring "substantial" identity between compared male and female jobs—does not limit an employer's liability for intentional wage discrimination under Title VII. For example, in *Miranda v. B & B Cash Grocery Store, Inc.*,[12] the plaintiff's inability to demonstrate that she performed the same work as higher paid males did not preclude a Title VII claim based on evidence male employees who performed fewer duties were paid more than she, or that the employer would have paid her more had she been a male. Thus, a violation of the EPA will generally violate Title VII, but the converse is not true.[13]

Additionally, the remedies for violation of the two laws differ. Under the EPA, a prevailing plaintiff may obtain backpay for any wages unlawfully withheld as the result of pay inequality and twice that amount in liquidated damages for a willful violation. By contrast, the Civil Rights Act of 1991 added to the backpay remedy authorized by Title VII a provision for jury trials and compensatory and punitive damages for victims of "intentional" sex discrimination in wage cases and otherwise.[14] Such damages may only be recovered, however, in cases of intentional discrimination, not in so-called "disparate impact" cases alleging the adverse effect of a facially neutral employment practice on a protected group member. In addition, the Title VII damages remedy is limited by dollar "caps," which vary depending on the size of the employer.[15]

"Comparable Worth" Litigation

During the 1980s, some litigants tried to substitute job equivalency for the "equal work standard" in the EPA through so-called comparable worth Title VII cases. As previously mentioned, whole classes of jobs are undervalued according to comparable worth theory because they traditionally have been predominately held by women. Because of alleged labor market bias against female-dominated jobs, Title VII plaintiffs contended that pay discrimination claims should not be limited by the EPA standard, requiring that jobs be substantially "equal" or similar for different pay rates to be considered discriminatory. Instead, Title VII wage-based discrimination actions against employers could be predicated on job evaluation studies, they argued, which compared the value of women's jobs to those of men who perform work that is dissimilar, but of equivalent or comparable worth to the employer.

Although not a comparable worth case, *County of Washington v. Gunther* held that the EPA's equal work standard was not a restriction on Title VII relief for intentional sex-based discrimination in pay between dissimilar male and female jobs.[16] But the Supreme Court did not speak specifically to the Title VII standard of proof for wage discrimination, since in *Gunther* the county's intention was clearly demonstrated by its failure to redress underpayment of wages to female employees revealed by its own pay evaluation study.

Outside of such "refusal to pay" cases, however, where no market surveys or pay evaluations were done, the courts have been reluctant to second-guess the wage rate dictated by the local labor market for dissimilar jobs. In a pair of decisions, the Ninth Circuit firmly rejected Title VII liability for a public employer's failure to pay equal wages to male and female employees allegedly performing comparable duties.

That case, *AFSCME v. State of Washington*,[17] held that the state lawfully paid employees in predominantly male job classifications more than it paid employees in predominantly female classifications, even though a state-commissioned study concluded that the male and female classifications were "comparable."

Reliance on market forces of supply and demand to set compensation for dissimilar male and female jobs was not *per se* illegal since "[n]either law nor logic deems the free market system a suspect enterprise." The state "may" have discretion to enact a comparable worth plan, the court held, but "Title VII does not obligate it to eliminate an economic inequality which it did not create."[18]

Earlier, in *Spaulding v. University of Washington*,[19] the same court denied a comparable worth claim by members of the female nursing faculty of the University of Washington who alleged that they were underpaid by comparison to other faculty departments.[20]

The *Ledbetter* Case and Subsequent Legislation

Meanwhile, in 2007 the Supreme Court issued a decision in *Ledbetter v. Goodyear Tire & Rubber Co., Inc.*,[21] a case in which the female plaintiff alleged that past sex discrimination had resulted in lower pay increases and that these past pay decisions continued to affect the amount of her pay throughout her employment, resulting in a significant pay disparity between her and her male colleagues by the end of her nearly 20-year career. Under Title VII, plaintiffs are required to file suit within 180 days "after the alleged unlawful employment practice occurred."[22] Although the plaintiff argued that each paycheck she received constituted a new violation of the statute and therefore reset the clock with regard to filing a claim, the Court rejected this argument, reasoning that "a new violation does not occur, and a new charging period does not commence, upon the occurrence of subsequent nondiscriminatory acts that entail adverse effects resulting from the past discrimination."[23] As a result, the Court held that the plaintiff had not filed suit in a timely manner. Initially, the decision appeared to limit some pay discrimination claims based on Title VII, but did not affect an individual's ability to sue for sex discrimination that results in pay bias under the Equal Pay Act, which does not contain the 180-day filing deadline.

Although the Court's decision made it more difficult for employees to sue for pay discrimination under Title VII, the ruling was subsequently superseded by the Lilly Ledbetter Fair Pay Act of 2009, which amended Title VII to clarify that the time limit for suing employers for pay discrimination begins each time they issue a paycheck and is not limited to the original discriminatory action.[24] This change is applicable not only to Title VII of the Civil Rights Act, but also to the Age Discrimination in Employment Act (ADEA), the Rehabilitation Act of 1973, and the Americans with Disabilities Act (ADA).

The *Wal-Mart* Case

In 2004, a federal district court permitted to proceed a class action on behalf of more than 1.5 million current and former female employees of Wal-Mart retail stores nationwide. In *Dukes et al. v. Wal-Mart Stores, Inc.*,[25] the plaintiffs claim that women over the past five years have been paid less than male workers in comparable positions and that the company systematically passed over female employees when awarding promotions to management.

According to two studies conducted by a sociologist and a statistician for the plaintiffs, 65% of Wal-Mart's hourly employees were women, but women make up only 33% of all management positions. The gender gap was even more striking when employment categories are further broken down; while the vast majority of Wal-Mart's cashiers are women, only a small fraction are store managers, the top in-store management position. The studies also found that women employed on a full-time hourly basis earned less per year on average than their male counterparts, and the shortfall was substantial for female store managers.

At this initial stage, the district court considered only whether the evidence raised issues of law and fact common to all members of the proposed class sufficient for a class action to proceed under federal law. The court did not decide the merits of plaintiffs' discrimination claims or any issue of Wal-Mart liability. In its opinion, however, the court noted:

> Plaintiffs present largely uncontested descriptive statistics which show that women working at Wal-Mart stores are paid less than men in every region, that pay disparities exist in most job categories, that the salary gap widens over time, that women take longer to enter management positions, and that the higher one looks in the organization the lower the percentage of women.[26]

Wal-Mart argued that any disparities were the result of decentralized decision-making at the regional and local level, not the result of any systematic employer bias, and that a massive class-action would be too large to administer. The court rejected that argument, however, noting that Title VII "contains no special exception for large employers." Moreover, "[i]nsulating our nation's largest employers from allegations that they have engaged in a pattern or practice of gender or racial discrimination—simply because they are large—would seriously undermine these imperatives."[27] Thus, any "inference" of discrimination in company compensation and promotion policies was found to "affect all plaintiffs in a common manner," and warranted the requested class certification.[28]

Wal-Mart appealed the district court's class action certification, and a three-judge panel of the appellate court upheld the class action certification,[29] as did a subsequent ruling by a divided panel of appellate judges sitting en banc.[30] In a 5-4 decision in *Wal-Mart v. Dukes*, however, the Supreme Court recently reversed the class certification ruling.[31]

Under the Federal Rules of Civil Procedure, parties seeking class certification must show, among other things, that "(1) the class is so numerous that joinder of all members is impracticable, (2) there are questions of law or fact common to the class, (3) the claims or defenses of the representative parties are typical of the claims or defenses of the class, and (4) the representative parties will fairly and adequately protect the interests of the class."[32]

According to the Court, the *Wal-Mart* plaintiffs failed to meet the commonality requirement because they could not establish that Wal-Mart operated under a common, general policy of discrimination. Rather: "The only corporate policy that the plaintiffs' evidence convincingly establishes is Wal-Mart's 'policy' of allowing discretion by local supervisors over employment matters. On its face, of course, that is just the opposite of a uniform employment practice that would provide the commonality needed for a class action."[33]

In its ruling, the Court emphasized that plaintiffs must provide "significant proof" that a "specific employment practice" led to the discrimination, and rejected as insufficient statistical and anecdotal evidence offered by the plaintiffs.[34] Although the Court's decision makes it more difficult for employees to receive class certification and thus makes it less likely that large employers will face similar suits in the future, it is not the end of the litigation. Plaintiffs may still pursue their claims as individuals, or perhaps as part of a smaller class. Indeed, some of the Wal-Mart plaintiffs have reportedly filed at least two new class action lawsuits against the company – one in California and one in Texas – but have limited their claims to stores located in a single state.[35]

Ultimately, if any of the claims against Wal-Mart go to trial, the female plaintiffs carry the burden of proving that the company engaged in an intentional pattern and practice of discriminating in pay and promotions. The record to date suggests that this may be no easy task, in part due to subjectivity in the company's personnel procedures and the fact that, prior to January 2003, the company apparently failed to post or document most available promotion opportunities.[36] There may be limited data on how many employees, male or female, applied for most of these positions. But if they prevail, whether at trial or by settlement, substantial monetary damages may be available to members of plaintiff class under Title VII.

Prior to the Court's decision in *Wal-Mart*, other large corporations that had been sued for pay discrimination had a tendency to enter into settlement agreements. For example, the investment firm Morgan Stanley reportedly agreed to pay $54 million to settle government claims that it systematically underpaid and failed to promote its women executives. Allegations of sexual harassment were also involved in the case. Beyond $12 million set aside to pay the lead plaintiff, a consent decree provides $40 million for any of about 340 other potential discrimination victims who are able to prove their claims, and another $2 million to establish internal anti-discrimination programs. For a period of three years, the decree required appointment of a firm ombudsman for sex discrimination issues and of an external monitor to review Morgan Stanley's adherence to the settlement and its progress at preventing discrimination.[37] Shortly after settlement in the Morgan Stanley case, both Boeing and Citigroup agreed to settle similar pay equity lawsuits, and Costco was sued for similar reasons.[38]

In contrast to the above corporations, Costco has chosen to defend itself in court. Although a federal district court granted class-action status to the plaintiffs in *Ellis v. Costco Wholesale Corp.*,[39] a federal appeals court subsequently vacated the district court's ruling regarding commonality and, specifically noting the Supreme Court's decision in *Wal-Mart v. Dukes*, remanded the case for reconsideration and application of the proper legal standard for evaluating commonality.[40] In the wake of the *Wal-Mart* decision, the *Ellis* plaintiffs are likely to have greater difficulty meeting the commonality requirements that are a prerequisite for receiving class certification.

RECENT LEGISLATION

Although the Ledbetter legislation discussed above is the only new pay discrimination law enacted by Congress in recent years, the issue of pay equity continues to garner congressional attention. Indeed, a number of measures have been introduced repeatedly in each of the last several congressional sessions. The two most prominent of these are the Paycheck Fairness Act and the Fair Pay Act, both of which are described below.

Paycheck Fairness Act

Introduced in each of the last several congressional sessions, the Paycheck Fairness Act (H.R. 1519/S. 3220 in the 112th Congress)[41] would increase penalties for employers who pay different wages to men and women for "equal work," and would add programs for training, research, technical assistance, and pay equity employer recognition awards. The legislation would also make it more difficult for employers to avoid EPA liability, and proposed safeguards would protect employees from retaliation for making inquiries or disclosures concerning employee wages and for filing a charge or participating in any manner in EPA proceedings. In short, while this legislation would adhere to current equal work standards of the EPA, it would reform the procedures and remedies for enforcing the law. In the 111th Congress, the House of Representatives passed both the Ledbetter legislation and the Paycheck Fairness Act as a combined package. The Senate, however, did not combine the two bills when it passed the Ledbetter legislation, and the Paycheck Fairness Act subsequently failed to pass in a procedural vote.

Under the EPA, as noted, prevailing plaintiffs may recover backpay in an amount equal to the total difference between wages actually received and those to which they are lawfully entitled and an additional amount equal to the backpay award as liquidated damages.[42] Compensatory damages are not authorized, and consequently, awards do not include sums for physical or mental distress, medical expenses, or other costs.[43] The Paycheck Fairness Act would authorize EPA class actions and "such compensatory and punitive damages as may be appropriate." In addition, the legislation would establish more restrictive standards for proof by employers of an affirmative defense to EPA liability based on any "bona fide factor other than sex." Thus, for a pay factor to be "bona fide," the employer would have to establish that it was "job related," consistent with "business necessity," and not derived from a sex-based differential in compensation, and that the employer's purpose could not be accomplished by less discriminatory alternative means.

Another aspect of EPA enforcement addressed by proposed pay equity bills concerns employer recordkeeping and the conduct of technical assistance, research, and educational programs by federal agencies. For example, the Paycheck Fairness Act would mandate record-keeping and data collection for better enforcement of the law. The measure would direct the Equal Employment Opportunity Commission (EEOC) to survey data currently available to the government and, in consultation with sister agencies, to identify additional sources of pay information that may be marshaled to support federal anti-discrimination efforts. The EEOC would be required to issue regulations for the collection of pay data from employers based on sex, race, and ethnicity, taking into consideration the burden placed on employers and the need to protect the confidentiality of required reports. In addition, the Secretary of Labor would be directed to develop job evaluation guidelines based on objective factors of education, skill, independence, and decision-making responsibility for *voluntary* use by employers in eliminating unfair pay disparities between traditionally male- and female-dominated occupations. Technical assistance and a recognition program would be awarded to employers who voluntarily adjust their wage scales pursuant to such a job evaluation. Finally, a "National Award for Pay Equity in the Workplace" would be established to recognize employers who demonstrate "substantial effort to eliminate pay disparities between men and women."

Fair Pay Act

The Fair Pay Act (H.R. 1493/S. 788 in the 112th Congress), which has predecessors dating back to the 103rd Congress, would go further than the Paycheck Fairness Act by proposing a fundamental expansion to the scope of the EPA, which is presently confined to sex-based wage differentials, by adding racial and ethnic minorities as protected classes under that law. Intentional wage discrimination against these groups is already prohibited by Title VII. But Title VII and the EPA have different standards of proof, and because proof of intent to discriminate is not required by the "equal pay for equal work" standard of the EPA,[44] it may provide greater protection to minority groups than Title VII in many cases. The EPA's catchall exception, affording employers broad immunity for pay differentials attributable to "factors other than sex," would be significantly narrowed by the Fair Pay Act. A compensatory and punitive damages remedy, without statutory limit, would replace the present EPA backpay and liquidated damages scheme, based on the Fair Labor Standards Act.

Significantly, the Fair Pay Act would also redefine the basic statutory standard of the EPA by requiring employers to pay equal wages regardless of sex, race, or national origin to workers in "equivalent jobs." Unlike the current law, Equal Pay Act claims based on wage disparities between dissimilar jobs—for example, a janitor and a clerk—would be permitted if they are determined to be "equivalent" in some largely undefined manner. By substituting job equivalency for the "equal work standard" in the EPA, the Fair Pay Act arguably could revive legal issues similar to those confronted by the federal courts during the 1980s in so-called "comparable worth" Title VII cases.

Finally, the Fair Pay Act would require all covered employers to maintain comprehensive records of "the method, system, calculations, and other bases used" to set employee wages and to file annual reports with the EEOC detailing the racial, ethnic, and gender composition of the employer's workforce broken down by job classification and wage or salary level. Such reports would be available for "reasonable" inspection and examination upon request of any person, pursuant to EEOC regulations, and could be used by the Commission for such "statistical and research purposes ... as it may deem appropriate." The EEOC would also be required to "carry on a continuing program of research, education, and technical assistance" to implement the proposed ban on racial, ethnic, or gender discrimination between employees working "in equivalent jobs."

End Notes

[1] 29 U.S.C. §206(d).

[2] 42 U.S.C. §§2000e et seq.

[3] All data in this section are from *Income, Poverty, and Health Insurance Coverage in the United States: 2010*, United States Census Bureau, September 2011, Table A-5, http://www.census.gov/prod/2011pubs/p60-239.pdf.

[4] Ibid. Table A-6. Earnings by educational attainment are limited to workers 25 years of age and over. Earnings by industry include all workers age 15 and over.

[5] The Women in Apprenticeship and Nontraditional Occupations Act (WANTO, P.L. 102-530) created one such program.

[6] See CRS Report 98-278, *The Gender Wage Gap and Pay Equity: Is Comparable Worth the Next Step?*, by Linda Levine, for information on the potential labor market effects of relying upon job evaluation as a wage-setting mechanism to implement comparable worth.

[7] See CRS Report 98-278, *The Gender Wage Gap and Pay Equity: Is Comparable Worth the Next Step?*, by Linda Levine, for a review of empirical analyses of the male-female wage gap.

[8] 29 U.S.C. §206(d)(1).

[9] *Id.*

[10] E.g. EEOC v. Madison Community United School District, 818 F.2d 577 (7th Cir. 1987)("equal work" requires a substantial identity rather than an absolute identity).

[11] 29 U.S.C. §206(d)(1).

[12] 975 F.2d 1518 (11th Cir. 1992).

[13] 29 C.F.R. §1620.27(a).

[14] 42 U.S.C. §1981A. Compensatory damages include "future pecuniary losses, emotional pain, suffering, inconvenience, mental anguish, loss of enjoyment of life and other nonpecuniary losses." Punitive damages may be recovered where the employer acted "with malice or with reckless indifference" to the complaining employee's federally protected rights.

[15] The sum total of compensatory and punitive damages awarded may not exceed $50,000 in the case of an employer with more than 14 and fewer than 101 employees; $100,000 in the case of an employer with more than 100 and fewer than 201 employees; $200,000 in the case of an employer with more than 200 and fewer than 500 employees; and $300,000 in the case of an employer with more than 500 employees.

[16] 452 U.S. 161 (1981).

[17] 770 F. 2d 1401 (9th Cir. 1985).

[18] *Id.* at 1407.

[19] 740 F. 2d 686 (9th Cir. 1984).

[20] See also American Nurses Ass'n v. State of Illinois, 606 F. Supp. 1313 (N.D.Ill. 1985)(Congress never intended to incorporate a comparable worth standard in Title VII and such a concept is neither sound nor workable).

[21] 550 U.S. 618 (2007).

[22] 42 U.S.C. §2000e-2(a)(1).

[23] Ledbetter v. Goodyear Tire & Rubber Co., 550 U.S. 618 (2007).

[24] P.L. 111-2.

[25] 222 F.R.D. 137 (N.D.Cal. 2004).

[26] *Id.* at 155.

[27] *Id.* at 142.

[28] *Id.* at 166.

[29] Dukes v. Wal-Mart, 509 F.3d 1168 (9th Cir. 2007).

[30] Dukes v. Wal-Mart Stores, Inc., 603 F.3d 571 (9th Cir. 2010).

[31] 131 S. Ct. 2541 (2011). The Court also unanimously held that claims for monetary relief may not be certified pursuant to Rule 23(b)(2), unless the monetary relief is incidental to the injunctive or declaratory relief. *Id.* at 2557.

[32] Fed. R. Civ. P. 23(a).

[33] Wal-Mart, 131 S. Ct. at 2554.

[34] *Id.* at 2553-56.

[35] Patrick Danner, "Floresville Woman Added to Suit," *San Antonio Express-News*, January 21, 2012, p. 2C.

[36] Dukes, 222 F.R.D. at 149.

[37] Brooke A. Masters, "Wall Street Sex-Bias Case Settled; Morgan Stanley Agrees to Pay $54 Million," *Washington Post*, July 13, 2004, at E01.

[38] Brooke A. Masters and Amy Joyce, "Costco is the Latest Class-Action Target; Lawyers' Interest Increases in Potentially Lucrative Discrimination Suits," *Washington Post*, August 18, 2004, at A01.

[39] 240 F.R.D. 627 (D. Cal. 2007).

[40] Ellis v. Costco Wholesale Corp., 657 F.3d 970 (9th Cir. 2011).

[41] S. 3220 is identical to S. 797, which was introduced earlier in the 112th Congress.

[42] 29 U.S.C. §§216-17.

[43] E.g. Hybki v. Alexander & Alexander, Inc., 536 F. Supp. 483 (W.D.Mo. 1982) (emphasizing damages for pain and suffering are not available under the EPA).

[44] See Fallon v. State of Illinois, 882 F.2d 1206 (7th Cir. 1989).

In: Sex Discrimination and Harassment   ISBN 978-1-62257-466-7
Editors: H. Andrews and S. Spencer   © 2012 Nova Science Publishers, Inc.

Chapter 5

TITLE IX, SEX DISCRIMINATION, AND INTERCOLLEGIATE ATHLETICS: A LEGAL OVERVIEW[*]

Jody Feder

SUMMARY

Enacted nearly four decades ago, Title IX of the Education Amendments of 1972 prohibits discrimination on the basis of sex in federally funded education programs or activities. Although the Title IX regulations bar recipients of federal financial assistance from discriminating on the basis of sex in a wide range of educational programs or activities, such as student admissions, scholarships, and access to courses, the statute is perhaps best known for prohibiting sex discrimination in intercollegiate athletics.

Indeed, the provisions regarding athletics have proved to be one of the more controversial aspects of Title IX. At the center of the debate is a three-part test that the Department of Education (ED) uses to determine whether institutions are providing nondiscriminatory athletic participation opportunities for both male and female students. Proponents of the existing regulations point to the dramatic increases in the number of female athletes in elementary and secondary school, college, and beyond as the ultimate indicator of the statute's success in breaking down barriers

---

[*] This is an edited, reformatted and augmented version of Congressional Research Service, Publication No. RL31709, dated December 17, 2010.

against women in sports. In contrast, opponents contend that the Title IX regulations unfairly impose quotas on collegiate sports and force universities to cut men's teams in order to remain in compliance. Critics further argue that the decline in certain men's sports, such as wrestling, is a direct result of Title IX's emphasis on proportionality in men's and women's college sports.

In 2002, ED appointed a commission to study Title IX and to recommend whether or not the athletics provisions should be revised. The Commission on Opportunity in Athletics delivered its final report to the Secretary of Education in 2003. In response, ED issued new guidance in 2003 and 2005 that clarified Title IX policy and the use of the three-part test.

This CRS report provides an overview of Title IX in general and the intercollegiate athletics regulations in particular, as well as a summary of the commission's report and ED's response and a discussion of legal challenges to the regulations and to the three-part test.

I. INTRODUCTION

Enacted nearly four decades ago, Title IX of the Education Amendments of 1972 prohibits discrimination on the basis of sex in federally funded education programs or activities.[1] Although the Title IX regulations bar recipients of federal financial assistance from discriminating on the basis of sex in a wide range of educational programs or activities, such as student admissions, scholarships, and access to courses, the statute is perhaps best known for prohibiting sex discrimination in intercollegiate athletics.

Indeed, the provisions regarding athletics have proved to be one of the more controversial aspects of Title IX. At the center of the debate is a three-part test that the Department of Education (ED) uses to determine whether institutions are providing nondiscriminatory athletic participation opportunities for both male and female students. Proponents of the existing regulations point to the dramatic increases in the number of female athletes in elementary and secondary school, college, and beyond as the ultimate indicator of the statute's success in breaking down barriers against women in sports. In contrast, critics contend that the Title IX regulations unfairly impose quotas on collegiate sports and force universities to cut men's teams in order to remain in compliance.[2] Critics further argue that the decline in certain men's sports, such as wrestling, is a direct result of Title IX's emphasis on proportionality in men's and women's college sports.

In 2002, ED appointed a commission to study Title IX and to recommend whether or not the athletics provisions should be revised.[3] The Commission on Opportunity in Athletics delivered its final report to the Secretary of Education in 2003.[4] In response, ED issued new guidance in 2003 and 2005 that clarified Title IX policy and the use of the three-part test.[5]

This CRS report provides an overview of Title IX in general and the intercollegiate athletics regulations in particular, as well as a summary of the commission's report and ED's response and a discussion of legal challenges to the regulations and to the three-part test.

II. TITLE IX BACKGROUND

Enacted in response to a growing concern regarding disparities in the educational experiences of male and female students, Title IX is designed to eliminate sex discrimination in education. Although Title IX prohibits a broad range of discriminatory actions, such as sexual harassment in elementary and secondary schools or discrimination against women in graduate school admissions, Title IX is perhaps best known for its role in barring discrimination against women in college sports. Indeed, when the Department of Health, Education, and Welfare (HEW), which was the predecessor agency of the Department of Education, issued policy guidance regarding Title IX and athletics, the agency specifically noted that participation rates for women in college sports "are far below those of men" and that "on most campuses, the primary problem confronting female athletes is the absence of a fair and adequate level of resources, services, and benefits."[6]

Federal law regarding Title IX intercollegiate athletics consists of three basic components: (1) the Title IX statute, which was enacted in the Education Amendments of 1972 and amended in the Education Amendments of 1974;[7] (2) the Department of Education regulations, which were originally issued in 1975 by HEW;[8] and (3) ED's policy guidance regarding Title IX athletics. The athletics policy guidance is primarily comprised of two documents: (1) a 1979 Policy Interpretation that established the controversial three-part test,[9] and (2) a 1996 Clarification of the three-part test, which reinvigorated enforcement of Title IX in intercollegiate athletics.[10] In addition, ED issued further clarifications in 2003 and 2005.[11] Despite the public attention generated by the three-part test, it is important to note that the test itself forms only a small part of the larger body of Title IX law. A general overview of the Title IX statute and regulations is provided below, while the athletics policy guidance and the legal debate surrounding Title IX and the three-part test are described in greater detail in subsequent sections.

In addition to this substantial body of Title IX law and policy, one other federal statute—the Equity in Athletics Disclosure Act[12]—also applies to intercollegiate athletics. Under this statute, colleges and universities are required to report statistical data, broken down by sex, on undergraduate enrollment and athletic participation and expenditures.

The Title IX Statute

Enacted nearly 40 years ago, the Title IX statute is designed to prevent sex discrimination by barring recipients of federal funds from discriminating in their education programs or activities. Specifically, the statute declares, "No person in the United States, shall, on the basis of sex, be excluded from participation in, be denied the benefits of, or be subjected to discrimination under any education program or activity receiving Federal financial assistance," subject to certain exceptions.[13]

The original Title IX legislation, which set forth the broad prohibition against sex discrimination but provided little detail about specific programs or activities, made no mention of college sports.

However, the Education Amendments of 1974 directed HEW to issue Title IX implementing regulations "which shall include with respect to intercollegiate athletic activities reasonable provisions considering the nature of particular sports."[14] This provision was added after Congress eliminated a section that would have made revenue-producing sports exempt from Title IX.[15]

It is important to note that, under Title IX, the receipt of any amount of federal financial assistance is sufficient to trigger the broad nondiscrimination obligation embodied in the statute. This nondiscrimination obligation extends institution-wide to *all* education programs or activities operated by the recipient of the federal funds, even if some of the education programs or activities themselves are not funded with federal dollars.[16] For example, virtually all colleges and universities in the United States are recipients of federal financial assistance because they receive some form of federal aid, such as scientific research grants or student tuition financed by federal loans. Once a particular school is deemed a recipient of federal financial assistance, all of the education programs and activities that it operates are subject to Title IX. Thus, if a college or university receives federal assistance through its student financial aid program, its nondiscrimination obligation is not restricted solely to its student financial aid program, but rather the obligation extends to all of the education programs or activities conducted by the institution, including athletics and other programs that do not receive federal funds. The provision regarding receipt of federal funds, therefore, is the primary mechanism for compelling institutions to comply with Title IX in their athletic programs.[17]

The Title IX Regulations

Because Title IX's prohibition against sex discrimination extends to all education programs or activities operated by recipients of federal funds, the scope of Title IX is quite broad. While the statute lays out only the general prohibition against sex discrimination, the implementing regulations specify the wide range of education programs or activities affected. Indeed, the regulations bar recipients from discriminating on the basis of sex in student admissions, recruitment, scholarship awards and tuition assistance, housing, access to courses and other academic offerings, counseling, financial assistance, employment assistance to students, health and insurance benefits and services, athletics, and all aspects of education-related employment, including recruitment, hiring, promotion, tenure, demotion, transfer, layoff, termination, compensation, benefits, job assignments and classifications, leave, and training.[18]

Despite the wide array of programs and activities subject to Title IX, it is the provisions on athletics that have generated the bulk of public attention and controversy in recent years. Under the Title IX regulations, recipients of federal financial assistance are prohibited from discriminating on the basis of sex in their sports programs. Specifically, the regulations declare, "No person shall, on the basis of sex, be excluded from participation in, be denied the benefits of, be treated differently from another person or otherwise be discriminated against in any interscholastic, intercollegiate, club or intramural athletics offered by a recipient."[19] In addition, recipients are barred from providing athletics separately on the basis of sex, except under certain circumstances, such as when team selection is based on competitive skill or the activity is a contact sport.[20] Finally, the regulations require institutions that provide athletic scholarships to make such awards available in proportion to the numbers of male and female students participating in intercollegiate athletics.[21]

An important principle embodied in the Title IX regulations on athletics is the principle of equal opportunity. Under the regulations, recipients such as colleges and universities must "provide equal athletic opportunity for members of both sexes."[22] When evaluating whether equal opportunities are available, the Department of Education (ED) examines, among other factors, the provision of equipment and supplies, scheduling of games and practice time, travel and per diem allowance, opportunity to receive coaching and academic tutoring, assignment and compensation of coaches and tutors, provision of locker rooms and practice and competitive facilities, provision of medical training facilities and services, provision of housing and dining facilities and services, and publicity.[23] In addition, ED considers "whether the selection of sports and levels of competition effectively accommodate the interests and abilities of members of both sexes."[24] In order to measure compliance with this last factor, ED established the three-part test that has been challenged by opponents of existing Title IX policy.

To clarify how to comply with the intercollegiate athletics requirements contained in the Title IX regulations, ED issued a Policy Interpretation in 1979 and a subsequent Clarification of this guidance in 1996.[25] Combined, these two documents form the substantive basis of the policy guidance on the three-part test, which has generated the bulk of the questions and concerns surrounding Title IX and intercollegiate athletics. ED also issued a further clarification in 2003, but this document made only minor alterations to the 1979 Policy Interpretation and the 1996 Clarification.[26] In addition, in 2005, ED issued yet another clarification that established a new way in which colleges may demonstrate compliance with the interest test prong of the three-part test.[27] These guidance documents are discussed in greater detail in the section below.

III. INTERCOLLEGIATE ATHLETICS AND THE POLICY GUIDANCE

As noted above, ED has set forth its interpretation of the intercollegiate athletics provisions of the Title IX statute and implementing regulations in two documents: the 1979 Policy Interpretation and the subsequent 1996 Clarification. These two documents, which remain in force, were designed to provide guidance to colleges and universities regarding how to achieve Title IX compliance by providing equal opportunity in their intercollegiate athletic programs. To that end, both of the guidance documents discuss the factors that ED considers when enforcing Title IX.[28]

Under the 1979 Policy Interpretation, HEW established three different standards to ensure equal opportunity in intercollegiate athletics.[29] First, with regard to athletic scholarships, the compliance standard is that such aid "should be available on a substantially proportional basis to the number of male and female participants in the institution's athletic program."[30] Second, HEW established a standard that male and female athletes should receive "equivalent treatment, benefits, and opportunities" in the following areas: equipment and supplies, games and practice times, travel and per diem, coaching and academic tutoring, assignment and compensation of coaches and tutors, locker rooms and practice and competitive facilities, medical and training facilities, housing and dining facilities, publicity, recruitment, and support services.[31] Finally, in terms of meeting the regulatory requirement to address the interests and abilities of male and female students alike, the compliance standard is that such interests and abilities must be equally effectively accommodated.[32]

In order to determine compliance with the latter accommodation standard, ED considers three additional factors: (1) the determination of athletic interests and abilities of students, (2) the selection of sports offered,[33] and (3) the levels of competition available, including the opportunity for team competition.[34] It is the criteria used to assess this third and final factor that form the basis of the three-part test. The three-part test, the debate over the test and its proportionality requirement, ED's Title IX review commission, and ED's response to the commission's report are discussed in detail below.

The Three-Part Test

Under the Policy Interpretation, in accommodating the interests and abilities of athletes of both sexes, institutions must provide the opportunity for male and female athletes to participate in competitive sports. ED measures an institution's compliance with this requirement through one of the following three methods:

(1) Whether intercollegiate level participation opportunities for male and female students are provided in numbers substantially proportionate to their respective enrollments; or (2) Where the members of one sex have been and are underrepresented among intercollegiate athletes,

whether the institution can show a history and continuing practice of program expansion, which is demonstrably responsive to the developing interest and abilities of the members of that sex ; or (3) Where the members of one sex are underrepresented among intercollegiate athletes, and the institution cannot show a continuing practice of program expansion such as that cited above, whether it can be demonstrated that the interests and abilities of the members of that sex have been fully and effectively accommodated by the present program.[35]

These three methods for determining whether institutions are complying with the Title IX requirement to provide nondiscriminatory participation opportunities for both male and female athletes have come to be referred to as the three-part test. In its 1996 Clarification, which addresses only the three-part test, ED provides additional guidance for institutions seeking to comply with Title IX.

According to the 1996 Clarification, an institution must meet only one part of the three-part test in order to prove its compliance with the nondiscrimination requirement.[36] Thus, institutions may prove compliance by meeting (1) the proportionality test, which measures whether the ratio of male and female athletes is substantially proportional to the ratio of male and female students at the institution, (2) the expansion test, which measures whether an institution has a history and continuing practice of expanding athletic opportunities for the underrepresented sex, or (3) the interests test, which measures whether an institution is accommodating the athletic interests of the underrepresented sex.[37]

In addition, the 1996 Clarification reiterates that ED examines many other factors beyond those set forth in the three-part test when it evaluates an institution's Title IX athletics compliance.[38] The 1996 Clarification also provides a more detailed examination of the factors that ED considers under each of the three tests, as well as examples illustrating how the various factors affect a finding of compliance or noncompliance.[39]

The 2003 Clarification and the 2005 Clarification, which provide additional guidance regarding the three-part test, are discussed separately below.

The Proportionality Test

The first prong of the three-part test—the proportionality test—is the most controversial. Indeed, critics contend that proportionality amounts to an unfair system of quotas. Because women's enrollment in postsecondary schools has increased dramatically in the decades since Title IX was enacted, rising 30% from 1981 to 1999,[40] critics argue that proportionality results in reverse discrimination, forcing schools to cut existing men's teams in order to create new slots for women.[41]

Proponents of proportionality respond that Title IX does not require quotas because schools that cannot demonstrate proportionality can still comply with Title IX if they pass one of the two remaining parts of the three-part test. Supporters also reject the notion that Title IX forces schools to eliminate men's teams, arguing that costly men's sports like football are to blame for cuts in less popular sports for both men and women. In addition, supporters note that instead of cutting men's sports, schools can achieve proportionality by adding women's teams.[42]

Critics counter that even though the three-part test offers an alternative to the proportionality approach in theory, in reality, maintaining proportionality is the only sure way to avoid a lawsuit. Furthermore, say critics, even though schools can technically comply with the proportionality standard by adding women's teams, budget realities often force institutions to cut men's teams instead. Proponents, however, respond that the vast majority of schools that add women's teams do not eliminate men's teams. Changing the proportionality test, say proponents, would be tantamount to repealing a law that is widely credited for dramatically increasing women's interest, participation, and success in sports.[43]

In 2001, the General Accounting Office (GAO) released a study of intercollegiate athletics. The GAO report included the following findings:

- "The number of women participating in intercollegiate athletics at 4-year colleges and universities increased substantially—from 90,000 to 163,000— between school years 1981-82 and 1998-99, while the number of men participating increased more modestly—from 220,000 to 232,000."[44]
- "Women's athletic participation grew at more than twice the rate of their growth in undergraduate enrollment, while men's participation more closely matched their growth in undergraduate enrollment."[45]
- "The total number of women's teams increased from 5,595 to 9,479, a gain of 3,784 teams, compared to an increase from 9,113 to 9,149 teams for men, a gain of 36 teams."[46]
- "Several women's sports and more than a dozen men's sports experienced net decreases in the number of teams. For women, the

largest net decreases in the number of teams occurred in gymnastics; for men, the largest decreases were in wrestling."[47]

- In men's sports, "the greatest increase in numbers of participants occurred in football, with about 7,200 more players. Football also had the greatest number of participants—approximately 60,000, or about twice as many as the next largest sport. Wrestling experienced the largest decrease in participation—a drop of more than 2,600 participants."[48]

- "In all, 963 schools added teams and 307 discontinued teams since 1992-93. Most were able to add teams—usually women's teams—without discontinuing any teams."[49]

- "Among the colleges and universities that added a women's team, the two factors cited most often as greatly influencing the decision were the need to address student interest in particular sports and the need to meet gender equity goals or requirements. Similarly, schools that discontinued a men's team cited a lack of student interest and gender equity concerns as the factors greatly influencing their decision, as well as the need to reallocate the athletic budget to other sports."[50]

ED's Interpretation of the Title IX Proportionality Test

Historically, ED has favored the proportionality approach to Title IX enforcement. Among the factors that ED considers under the proportionality test are the number of participation opportunities provided to athletes of both sexes. According to ED, "as a general rule, all athletes who are listed on a team's squad or eligibility list and are on the team as of the team's first competitive event are counted as participants."[51] ED next determines whether these participation opportunities are substantially proportionate to the ratio of male and female students enrolled at the institution, but, for reasons of flexibility, ED does not require exact proportionality.[52]

According to the 1996 Clarification, the proportionality test acts as a safe harbor. In other words, if an institution can demonstrate proportional athletic opportunities for women, then the institution will automatically be found to be in compliance.[53] If, however, an institution cannot prove proportionality, then the institution can still establish compliance by demonstrating that the imbalance does not reflect discrimination because the institution either (1) has a demonstrated history and continuing practice of expanding women's sports opportunities (prong two) or (2) has fully and effectively accommodated the athletic interests of women (prong three).

In its 2003 Clarification, ED specifically addressed the "safe harbor" language in the 1996 guidance. Noting that the "safe harbor" phrase had led many schools to believe erroneously that achieving compliance with Title IX could be guaranteed by meeting the proportionality test only, ED reiterated that "each of the three prongs of the test is an equally sufficient means of complying with Title IX, and no one prong is favored."[54]

Finally, the 1996 Clarification explicitly declares that "nothing in the three-part test requires an institution to eliminate participation opportunities for men" and challenges the notion that the three-part test requires quotas.[55] Rather, the 1996 Clarification states that "the three-part test gives institutions flexibility and control over their athletic programs."[56] Furthermore, the 1996 Clarification notes that the Policy Interpretation in general and the three-part test in particular have been upheld by every court that has reviewed the guidance documents.[57]

The Title IX Review Commission

Although ED has enforced its Title IX policy, including the three-part test and its proportionality standard, virtually unchanged since shortly after the statute was enacted nearly four decades ago, several years ago the agency considered whether or not to alter its athletics policy. To that end, ED appointed the Commission on Opportunity in Athletics in June 2002 to review Title IX and to recommend changes if warranted. The commission, which held a series of meetings around the country to discuss problems with and improvements to Title IX, issued its final report containing findings and recommendations in February 2003.[58]

In its report, the commission noted that it "found strong and broad support for the original intent of Title IX, coupled with a great deal of debate over how the law should be enforced," but that "more needs to be done to create opportunities for women and girls and retain opportunities for boys and men."[59] Ultimately, the final report contained 23 recommendations for strengthening Title IX, including 15 recommendations that were adopted unanimously. When the commission issued its final report, however, two dissenting members of the panel refused to sign the document and instead issued a minority report in which they withdrew their support for two of the unanimous recommendations and raised concerns about several other unanimous recommendations.[60] The Secretary of Education indicated that he intended to consider changes only with respect to the unanimous recommendations of the commission.

Among the unanimous recommendations of the commission were suggestions that ED (1) reaffirm its commitment to eliminating discrimination; (2) clarify its guidance and promote consistency in enforcement; (3) avoid making changes to Title IX that undermine enforcement; (4) clarify that cutting teams in order to achieve compliance is a disfavored practice; (5) enforce Title IX aggressively by implementing sanctions against violators; (6) promote student interest in athletics at elementary and secondary schools; (7) support amendments to the Equity in Athletics Disclosure Act that would improve athletic reporting requirements; (8) disseminate information on the criteria it uses to help schools determine whether activities that they offer qualify as athletic opportunities; (9) encourage the National Collegiate Athletic Association to review its scholarship and other guidelines; (10) advise schools that walk-on opportunities are not limited for schools that comply with the second or third prong of the three-part test; (11) examine the prospect of allowing institutions to demonstrate compliance with the third prong of the three-part test by comparing the ratio of male and female athletic participation with the demonstrated interests and abilities shown by regional, state, or national youth or high school participation rates or by interest levels indicated in student surveys; (12) abandon the "safe harbor" designation for the proportionality test in favor of treating each of the three tests equally; and (13) consider revising the second prong of the three-part test, possibly by designating a point at which a school can no longer establish compliance through this part.[61]

The commission originally adopted an additional two recommendations unanimously, but the two dissenting members of the panel withdrew their support for these recommendations upon further opportunity for review of the final report. These contested recommendations suggested that ED (1) clarify the meaning of "substantial proportionality" to allow for a reasonable variance in the ratio of men's and women's athletic participation; and (2) explore additional ways of demonstrating equity beyond the three-part test.[62]

Other recommendations that the commission adopted by a majority, but not unanimous, vote included suggestions that ED (1) adopt any future changes to Title IX through the normal federal rulemaking process; (2) encourage the reduction of excessive expenditures in intercollegiate athletics, possibly by exploring an antitrust exemption for college sports; (3) inform universities about the current requirements governing private funding of certain sports; (4) reexamine its requirements governing private funding of certain sports to allow such funding of sports that would otherwise be cut; (5) allow schools to comply with the proportionality test by counting the available slots on sports teams rather than actual participants; (6) for purposes of the proportionality test, exclude from the participation count walk-on athletes, who are non-scholarship players that tend to be male; (7) allow schools to conduct interest surveys to demonstrate compliance with the three-part test; and (8) for purposes of the proportionality test, exclude nontraditional students, who tend to be female, from the count of enrolled students. In addition, the commission was evenly divided on a recommendation that would allow schools to meet the proportionality test if athletic participation rates were 50% male and 50% female, with a variance of two to three percentage points allowed.[63]

ED's Response to the Title IX Commission: The 2003 and 2005 Clarifications

In response to the commission's report, ED indicated that it would study the recommendations and consider whether or not to revise its Title IX athletics policy. Several months later, ED issued new guidance that essentially left the existing Title IX policy unchanged. In its 2003 Clarification, which provided further guidance regarding Title IX policy and the three-part test, ED reiterated that all three prongs of the three-part test have been and can be used to demonstrate compliance with Title IX, and the agency encouraged schools to use the approach that best suits its needs. In addition, the 2003 Clarification declared that complying with Title IX does not require schools to cut teams and that eliminating teams is a disfavored practice. The 2003 Clarification also noted that ED expects both to provide technical assistance to schools and to aggressively enforce Title IX. Finally, the guidance indicated that ED will continue to allow private sponsorship of athletic teams.[64]

In 2005, ED issued yet another clarification of the three-part test.[65] In the 2005 Clarification, ED provided additional guidance with respect to part three of the three-part test. Under that test, known as the interests test, an institution may demonstrate compliance with Title IX by establishing that it is accommodating the athletic interests of the underrepresented sex. The new guidance clarified that one of the ways in which schools may demonstrate compliance with the interests test is by using an online survey to establish that the underrepresented sex has no unmet interests in athletic participation. Such a survey must be administered periodically to all students that are members of the underrepresented sex, and students must be informed that a failure to respond to the survey will be viewed as an indication of a lack of interest. As a result, the survey must be administered in a way designed to generate high response rates.

The 2005 Clarification emphasized that schools have flexibility to demonstrate compliance under any one part of the three-part test and that schools who choose to demonstrate compliance through the interests test have the option to do so in several ways. Among the factors that ED considers when determining whether the school has accurately measured student interest are surveys, requests for the addition of a varsity team, participation in club or intramural sports, participation rates in local high schools and athletic organizations, and intercollegiate participation rates in the school's region. Even if a school's population of the underrepresented sex is found to have an unmet interest in sports, the institution will not be found to have violated Title IX unless ED also finds that there is sufficient ability to sustain a team and a reasonable expectation of intercollegiate competition in the sport within the school's normal competitive region.[66]

IV. TITLE IX AND THE COURTS

Over the years, the Supreme Court has heard several cases pertaining to Title IX. Until 2005, none of these cases had involved college or high school sports, but they did help to shape the legal landscape surrounding Title IX athletics policy. For example, in 1979, the Supreme Court held that Title IX includes a private right of action.[67] This decision strengthened Title IX enforcement because it means that an individual can sue in court for violations under the statute rather than wait for ED to pursue a complaint administratively. The Court further strengthened Title IX enforcement in 1992, when it ruled that individuals could sue for money damages in a Title IX lawsuit.[68] Finally, in a decision that was later overturned by Congress, the Court ruled that Title IX did not apply to an entire educational institution but rather applied only to the portion of the institution that received federal funds.[69]

In 2005, the Court handed down its decision in *Jackson v. Birmingham Board of Education*.[70] In this case, which involved a girl's basketball coach who claimed that he was removed from his coaching position in retaliation for his complaints about unequal treatment of the girl's team, the Court held that Title IX not only encompasses retaliation claims, but also is available to individuals who complain about sex discrimination, even if such individuals themselves are not the direct victims of sex discrimination.[71] Reasoning that "Title IX's enforcement scheme would unravel" "if retaliation went unpunished,"[72] the Court concluded that "when a funding recipient retaliates against a person because he complains of sex discrimination, this constitutes intentional discrimination on the basis of sex in violation of Title IX.[73]

Although the Supreme Court has decided only one case that directly involves Title IX athletics, the lower federal courts have heard multiple challenges to the statute and regulations. In fact, all of the federal courts of appeals that have considered the athletics Policy Interpretation, the three-part test, and the proportionality rule have upheld ED's Title IX regulations and policy.[74] In general, these courts have noted that the regulations and guidance represent a reasonable agency interpretation of Title IX, and they have ruled that the three-part test does not unfairly impose quotas because institutions may select from two other methods besides proportionality in order to comply with Title IX. Indeed, in 1993, the First Circuit reached this conclusion in *Cohen v. Brown University*, a landmark Title IX case that was the first federal appeals court decision regarding Title IX athletics.[75] This section provides a brief summary of the *Cohen* decision, as well as a description of the National Wrestling Coaches Association lawsuit, which has been dismissed, and more recent cases involving the question of whether high school sports associations discriminate when they schedule boys and girls' sports in different seasons.

Cohen v. Brown University

In the *Cohen* case, female athletes at Brown University sued under Title IX when the school eliminated two women's sports—gymnastics and volleyball—and two male teams—golf and water polo—in a cost-cutting measure.[76] Although the cuts made far larger reductions in the women's athletic budget than in the men's, the cuts did not affect the ratio of male to female athletes, which remained roughly 63% male to 37% female, despite a student body that was approximately 52% male and 48% female.[77] In their lawsuit, the members of the women's gymnastics and volleyball teams "charged that Brown's athletic arrangements violated Title IX's ban on gender-based discrimination."[78] When the district court ordered the university to reinstate the two women's teams pending a full trial on the merits, Brown appealed by challenging the validity of both the Title IX guidance in general and the three-part test in particular. The First Circuit, however, affirmed the district court's decision in favor of the female athletes.[79]

In reaching its decision to uphold the validity of the three-part test, the First Circuit emphasized that ED's interpretation of Title IX warranted deference. According to the court, "the degree of deference is particularly high in Title IX cases because Congress explicitly delegated to the agency the task of prescribing standards for athletic programs under Title IX."[80] Thus, the court adopted ED's three-part test as an acceptable standard by which to measure an institution's compliance with Title IX, as have all other appeals courts to subsequently consider the issue.[81]

Next, the court in *Cohen* turned to the question of whether the university had met any one part of the three-part test. Because there was a large disparity between the proportion of women at Brown who were students versus the proportion who were athletes and because the university had not demonstrated a history of expanding women's sports, the court focused its inquiry on whether or not Brown had met part three of the test by effectively accommodating student interest. The university argued that when measuring interest under this standard, the relative athletic interests of male and female students should be the proper point of comparison rather than the relative enrollment of male and female students.[82] In effect, Brown argued that its female students were less interested in sports than its male students and that its Title IX compliance should thus be measured by this standard.

Under ED's construction of the accommodation test, however, institutions must ensure participation opportunities where there is "sufficient interest and ability among the members of the excluded sex to sustain a viable team and a reasonable expectation of intercollegiate competition for that team."[83] Noting that this standard does not require institutions to provide additional athletic opportunities every time female students express interest, the court upheld the district court's finding that the existence and success of women's gymnastics and volleyball at Brown demonstrated that there was sufficient interest in and expectation of competition in those sports to rule in favor of the female athletes with regard to the third prong of the three-part test.[84] In a subsequent appeal in the *Cohen* case, the court explicitly noted that Brown's view of the accommodation test, which seems to assume that women are naturally less interested in sports than men, reflects invidious gender stereotypes and could potentially freeze in place any existing disparity in athletic participation.[85]

Finally, the court rejected the university's constitutional challenge, ruling that Title IX does not violate the Equal Protection clause of the Fourteenth

Amendment.[86] In a subsequent appeal in the *Cohen* case, the court emphasized this point:

> No aspect of the Title IX regime at issue in this case – inclusive of the statute, the relevant regulation, and the pertinent agency documents – mandates gender-based preferences or quotas, or specific timetables for implementing numerical goals.... Race- and gender-conscious remedies are both appropriate and constitutionally permissible under a federal anti-discrimination regime, although such remedial measures are still subject to equal protection review.[87]

Challenges to Sports Scheduling Decisions

More recently, some parents and students have begun filing lawsuits that challenge the decision of certain state high school sports associations to schedule girls' sports in nontraditional seasons that differ from the season for corresponding boys' sports, arguing that the scheduling disparity violates the Equal Protection clause of the Constitution and Title IX. In Michigan, for example, a federal district court ruled that the Michigan High School Athletic Association's (MHSAA) scheduling of high school sports seasons in Michigan discriminated against female athletes on the basis of gender and thus violated the Constitution and Title IX.[88] Without reaching the statutory Title IX argument, the U.S. Court of Appeals for the Sixth Circuit upheld the district court on constitutional grounds.[89] Although this type of Title IX lawsuit appears to have emerged only in recent years, similar legal challenges have occurred in other states.[90]

The National Wrestling Coaches Association Lawsuit

Meanwhile, disturbed by the decline in the number of men's wrestling teams at colleges and universities across the country, the National Wrestling Coaches Association (NWCA), together with former wrestling teams at several institutions, filed a lawsuit against ED in 2002, arguing that the Title IX regulations were adopted illegally and that Title IX unfairly discriminates against men.[91] In the lawsuit, the NWCA argued (1) that ED's establishment of the Title IX regulations and policy guidance was procedurally defective, (2) that ED exceeded its authority under the Title IX statute when enacting those regulations and guidance, and (3) that ED's regulations and guidance discriminate against male athletes, thereby violating the Title IX statute and the Equal Protection clause of the Fourteenth Amendment.[92]

In response to the lawsuit, ED, backed by the Bush Administration, moved to dismiss the case on the grounds that (1) the plaintiffs lacked standing to bring the case; (2) judicial review was unauthorized under the circumstances of this particular case; and (3) the suit was barred by the statute of limitations.[93] The National Women's Law Center (NWLC) filed an amicus brief in support of ED, arguing that the suit was improper because there was no guarantee that institutions would reinstate men's sports teams even if the Title IX regulations and policy were changed. The NWLC further observed that arguments similar to those made in the NWCA lawsuit had been rejected by every federal appeals court to consider the issue of Title IX.[94] Ultimately, the NWCA lawsuit was dismissed from federal court on the grounds that the plaintiffs lacked the proper standing to bring the case.[95] The dismissal was affirmed by an appeals court,[96] and the Supreme Court effectively upheld the dismissal when it refused to review the case.[97]

Given the results in the NWCA case and in other Title IX cases brought before the federal courts of appeals, it seems likely that the courts will continue to defer to ED with regard to Title IX athletics policy in the near future. As noted above, ED has indicated that it intends to continue to use the three-part test to enforce Title IX. However, Congress could, if it disapproves of ED's Title IX athletics policy, respond with legislation to override the current regulations and guidance.

End Notes

[1] 20 U.S.C. §§ 1681 et seq.

[2] June Kronholz, *College Coaches Press Bush on Title IX*, The Wall Street Journal, Aug. 27, 2002, at A4.

[3] Erik Brady, *Major Changes Debated for Title IX*, USA Today, Dec. 18, 2002, at A1.

[4] The Secretary of Education's Commission on Opportunity in Athletics, *"Open to All": Title IX at Thirty*, Feb. 28, 2003, http://www.ed.gov/about/bdscomm/list/athletics/report.html.

[5] Department of Education, Further Clarification of Intercollegiate Athletics Policy Guidance Regarding Title IX Compliance (July 11, 2003) (hereinafter 2003 Clarification); Department of Education, Additional Clarification on Intercollegiate Athletics Policy: Three-Part Test—Part Three (March 17, 2005) (hereinafter 2005 Clarification).

[6] Title IX of the Education Amendments of 1972; A Policy Interpretation: Title IX and Intercollegiate Athletics, 44 FR 71413, 71419 (Dec. 11, 1979) (hereinafter 1979 Policy Interpretation).

[7] P.L. 93-380.

[8] 34 CFR Part 106.

[9] 1979 Policy Interpretation, *supra* footnote 6, at 71413.

[10] Department of Education, Clarification of Intercollegiate Athletics Policy Guidance: The Three-Part Test (Jan. 16, 1996) (hereinafter 1996 Clarification).

[11] 2003 Clarification, *supra* footnote 5; 2005 Clarification, *supra* footnote 5.

[12] 20 U.S.C. § 1092(g).

[13] *Id.* at § 1681(a). Exceptions include admissions to elementary and secondary schools, educational institutions of religious organizations with contrary religious tenets, military training institutions, educational institutions that are traditionally single-sex, fraternities and sororities, certain voluntary youth service organizations such as the Girl or Boy Scouts, father-son or mother-daughter activities at educational institutions, and beauty pageants. *Id.*

[14] P.L. 93-380 § 844.

[15] 1979 Policy Interpretation, *supra* footnote 6, at 71413.

[16] Department of Justice, Civil Rights Division, Title IX Legal Manual 51 (Jan. 11, 2001), *available at* http://www.usdoj.gov/crt/cor/coord/ixlegal.pdf.

[17] For a brief period from 1984 to 1988, Title IX enforcement in college athletics was suspended as a result of a Supreme Court ruling that Title IX was "program-specific," meaning that the statute's requirements applied only to education programs that received federal funds and not to an institution's programs as a whole. Grove City College v. Bell, 465 U.S. 555, 574 (1984). Because few university athletic programs receive federal dollars, college sports were essentially exempt from Title IX coverage after this decision. In the Civil Rights Restoration Act of 1987 (P.L. 100- 259), however, Congress overrode the Supreme Court's interpretation of Title IX by passing legislation to clarify that Title IX's requirements apply institution-wide and are not program-specific, thus reinstating Title IX's coverage of athletics. 20 U.S.C. § 1687.

[18] 34 CFR §§ 106.31-106.56.

[19] *Id.* at § 106.41(a).

[20] *Id.* at §106.41(b). Under the regulations, contact sports are defined to include boxing, wrestling, rugby, ice hockey, football, and basketball.

[21] *Id.* at § 106.37(c).

[22] *Id.* at § 106.41(c).

[23] *Id.*

[24] *Id.*

[25] 1979 Policy Interpretation, *supra* footnote 6; 1996 Clarification, *supra* footnote 10.

[26] 2003 Clarification, *supra* footnote 5.

[27] 2005 Clarification, *supra* footnote 5.

[28] 1979 Policy Interpretation, *supra* footnote 6; 1996 Clarification, *supra* footnote 10.

[29] Although the Policy Interpretation focuses on formal intercollegiate athletic programs, its requirements also apply to club, intramural, and interscholastic athletics. 1979 Policy Interpretation, *supra* footnote 6.

[30] *Id.* at 71414. This requirement, however, does not mean that schools must provide a proportional number of scholarships or that all individual scholarships must be of equal value; the only requirement is that the overall amount spent on scholarship aid must be proportional. *Id.* at 71415.

[31] *Id.* Such benefits, opportunities, and treatment need not be identical, and even a finding of nonequivalence can be justified by a showing of legitimate nondiscriminatory factors. According to the Policy Interpretation, "some aspects of athletic programs may not be equivalent for men and women because of unique aspects of particular sports or athletic

activities." The Policy Interpretation specifically cites football as an example of such a sport. *Id.*at 71415-16.

[32] *Id.* at 71414.

[33] According to the Policy Interpretation, "the regulation does not require institutions to integrate their teams nor to provide exactly the same choice of sports to men and women. However, where an institution sponsors a team in a particular sport for members of one sex, it may be required either to permit the excluded sex to try out for the team or to sponsor a separate team for the previously excluded sex." *Id.* at 71417-18.

[34] *Id.* at 71417.

[35] *Id.* at 71418.

[36] 1996 Clarification, *supra* footnote 10.

[37] Dear Colleague Letter from the Department of Education's Office for Civil Rights regarding the Clarification of Intercollegiate Athletics Policy Guidance: The Three-Part Test (Jan. 16, 1996), *available at* http://www.ed.gov/about/ offices/list/ocr/docs/clarific.html (hereinafter Dear Colleague Letter).

[38] 1996 Clarification, *supra* footnote 10.

[39] *Id.*

[40] General Accounting Office, Intercollegiate Athletics: Four-Year Colleges' Experiences Adding and Discontinuing Teams 8 (March 2001).

[41] Brady, *supra* footnote 3.

[42] *Id.*

[43] *Id.*

[44] General Accounting Office, Intercollegiate Athletics: Four-Year Colleges' Experiences Adding and Discontinuing Teams 4 (March 2001).

[45] *Id.*

[46] *Id.*

[47] *Id.*

[48] *Id.* at 10.

[49] *Id.* at 5.

[50] *Id.*

[51] 1996 Clarification, *supra* footnote 10.

[52] *Id.*

[53] Dear Colleague Letter, *supra* footnote 37.

[54] 2003 Clarification, *supra* footnote 5.

[55] 1996 Clarification, *supra* footnote 10.

[56] *Id.*

[57] Dear Colleague Letter, *supra* footnote 37. For a brief review of significant Title IX court decisions, see the "Title IX and the Courts" section below.

[58] The Secretary of Education's Commission on Opportunity in Athletics, *"Open to All": Title IX at Thirty*, Feb. 28, 2003, http://www.ed.gov/about/bdscomm/list/athletics/report.html.

[59] *Id.* at 4, 21.

[60] Donna de Varona and Julie Foudy, *Minority Views on the Report of the Commission on Opportunity in Athletics*, Feb. 2003, http://www.nwlc.org/pdf/MinorityReportFeb26.pdf.

[61] The Secretary of Education's Commission on Opportunity in Athletics, *"Open to All": Title IX at Thirty*, Feb. 28, 2003, 33-40, http://www.ed.gov/about/bdscomm/list/athletics/report.html.

[62] Donna de Varona and Julie Foudy, *Minority Views on the Report of the Commission on Opportunity in Athletics*, Feb. 2003, http://www.nwlc.org/pdf/MinorityReportFeb26.pdf.

63 The Secretary of Education's Commission on Opportunity in Athletics, *"Open to All": Title IX at Thirty*, Feb. 28, 2003, 33-40, http://www.ed.gov/about/bdscomm/list/athletics/report.html.

64 2003 Clarification, *supra* footnote 5.

65 2005 Clarification, *supra* footnote 5.

66 *Id.*

67 Cannon v. Univ. of Chicago, 441 U.S. 677 (1979).

68 Franklin v. Gwinnett County Public Schools, 503 U.S. 60 (1992).

69 Grove City College v. Bell, 465 U.S. 555 (1984). *See also supra* notes 16-17 and accompanying text.

70 125 S.Ct. 1497 (2005).

71 *Id.* at 1502.

72 *Id.* at 1508.

73 *Id.* at 1504 [internal quotations omitted].

74 *See, e.g.*, Chalenor v. Univ. of North Dakota, 291 F.3d 1042 (8th Cir. 2002); Pederson v. Louisiana State Univ., 213 F.3d 858 (5th Cir. 2000); Neal v. Bd. of Trustees, 198 F.3d 763 (9th Cir. 1999); Horner v. Kentucky High Sch. Athletic Ass'n, 43 F.3d 265 (6th Cir. 1994); Kelley v. Bd. of Trustees, 35 F.3d 265(7th Cir. 1994), *cert. denied*, 513 U.S. 1128; Williams v. Sch. Dist. of Bethlehem, 998 F.2d 168 (3d Cir. 1993); Roberts v. Colorado State Bd. of Agric., 998 F.2d 824 (10th Cir. 1993), *cert. denied*, 510 U.S. 1004; Cohen v. Brown Univ., 991 F.2d 888 (1st Cir. 1993) (hereinafter Cohen I). In addition, in a second appeal on a separate issue in the *Cohen* case, the First Circuit strongly reiterated its previous ruling upholding Title IX. Cohen v. Brown Univ., 101 F.3d 155 (1st Cir. 1996), *cert. denied*, 520 U.S. 1186 (hereinafter Cohen II).

75 991 F.2d 888, 891 (1st Cir. 1993).

76 *Id.* at 892.

77 *Id.*

78 *Id* at 893.

79 *Id.* at 891.

80 *Id.* at 895.

81 *See, e.g.*, Chalenor v. Univ. of North Dakota, 291 F.3d 1042 (8th Cir. 2002); Pederson v. Louisiana State Univ., 213 F.3d 858 (5th Cir. 2000); Neal v. Bd. of Trustees, 198 F.3d 763 (9th Cir. 1999); Horner v. Kentucky High Sch. Athletic Ass'n, 43 F.3d 265 (6th Cir. 1994); Kelley v. Bd. of Trustees, 35 F.3d 265(7th Cir. 1994), *cert. denied*, 513 U.S. 1128; Williams v. Sch. Dist. of Bethlehem, 998 F.2d 168 (3d Cir. 1993); Roberts v. Colorado State Bd. of Agric., 998 F.2d 824 (10th Cir. 1993), *cert. denied*, 510 U.S. 1004; Cohen v. Brown Univ., 991 F.2d 888 (1st Cir. 1993) (Cohen I). In addition, in a second appeal on a separate issue in the *Cohen* case, the First Circuit strongly reiterated its previous ruling upholding Title IX. Cohen v. Brown Univ., 101 F.3d 155 (1st Cir. 1996), *cert. denied*, 520 U.S. 1186 (Cohen II).

82 Cohen I, 991 F.2d at 899.

83 1979 Policy Interpretation, *supra* footnote 6, at 71418.

84 Cohen I, 991 F.2d at 904.

85 Cohen II, 101 F.3d 155, 176.

86 Cohen I, 991 F.2d at 900-01.

87 Cohen II, 101 F.3d at 170, 172.

88 Cmtys. for Equity v. Michigan High Sch. Athletic Ass'n, 178 F. Supp. 2d 805 (W.D.Mich.2001).

[89] Cmtys. for Equity v. Mich. High School Athletic Ass'n, 377 F. 3d 504 (6th Cir. 2004). The Supreme Court vacated and remanded the Sixth Circuit decision, Mich. High School Athletic Ass'n v. Cmtys. for Equity, 544 U.S. 1012 (2005), but the Sixth Circuit upheld its decision on remand. Cmtys. for Equity v. Mich. High School Athletic Ass'n, 459 F.3d 676 (6th Cir. 2006), *cert. denied*, Mich. High Sch. Ath. Ass'n v. Cmtys. for Equity, 127 S. Ct. 1912 (2007).

[90] *Review is Sought on Girls' Sports Ruling*, Wash. Post, May 3, 2005, at D02.

[91] Lori Nickel and Nahal Toosi, *Title IX is Taken To Task*, Milwaukee Journal Sentinel, Jan. 17, 2002 at C1.

[92] Complaint for Declaratory and Injunctive Relief, Nat'l Wrestling Coaches Ass'n v. Dep't of Educ., Civil Action No. 1:02CV00072-EGS, available at http://www.nwcaonline.com.

[93] Defendant's Motion to Dismiss, Nat'l Wrestling Coaches Ass'n v. Dep't of Educ., Civil Action No. 1:02CV00072- EGS, available at http://www.ed.gov/news/pressreleases/2002/05/wrestling.dismiss.mem.fin.pdf.

[94] Brief of Amici Curiae, Nat'l Wrestling Coaches Ass'n v. Dep't of Educ., Civil action No. 1:02CV00072-EGS, *available at* http://www.nwlc.org/pdf/amicusbrief.final.pdf.

[95] Nat'l Wrestling Coaches Ass'n v. Dep't of Educ., 263 F. Supp. 2d 82, at 129-30 (D.D.C. June 11, 2003).

[96] Nat'l Wrestling Coaches Ass'n v. Dep't of Educ., 361 U.S. App. D.C. 257 (D.C. Cir. May 14, 2004).

[97] Nat'l Wrestling Coaches Ass'n v. Dep't of Educ., 545 U.S. 1104 (U.S. 2005).

In: Sex Discrimination and Harassment   ISBN 978-1-62257-466-7
Editors: H. Andrews and S. Spencer   © 2012 Nova Science Publishers, Inc.

Chapter 6

TITLE IX AND SINGLE SEX EDUCATION: A LEGAL ANALYSIS[*]

Jody Feder

SUMMARY

Under Title IX of the Education Amendments of 1972, which prohibits sex discrimination in federally funded education programs or activities, school districts have long been permitted to operate single-sex schools. In 2006, the Department of Education (ED) published Title IX regulations that, for the first time, authorized schools to establish single-sex classrooms as well. This report evaluates the regulations in light of statutory requirements under Title IX and the Equal Educational Opportunities Act (EEOA) and in consideration of constitutional equal protection requirements.

Enacted over three decades ago, Title IX of the Education Amendments of 1972 prohibits discrimination on the basis of sex in federally funded education programs or activities.[1] Although Title IX bars recipients of federal financial assistance from discriminating on the basis of sex in a wide range of educational programs or activities, both the statute and the implementing regulations have long permitted school districts to operate single-sex schools.

---

[*] This is an edited, reformatted and augmented version of Congressional Research Service, Publication No. RS22544, dated December 15, 2008.

In 2006, however, the Department of Education (ED) issued Title IX regulations that, for the first time, authorized schools to operate individual classes on a single-sex basis.[2] The issuance of these regulations has raised a number of legal questions regarding whether single-sex classrooms pose constitutional problems under the equal protection clause or conflict with statutory requirements under Title IX or under the Equal Educational Opportunity Act (EEOA).[3]

BACKGROUND

Under Title IX, "No person ... shall, on the basis of sex, be excluded from participation in, be denied the benefits of, or be subjected to discrimination under any education program or activity receiving Federal financial assistance."[4] Although the statute prohibits a broad range of discriminatory actions, such as bias in college sports and sexual harassment in schools, Title IX does contain several exceptions. One of these exceptions provides that, with respect to admissions, Title IX applies only to institutions of vocational education, professional education, and graduate higher education, and to public institutions of undergraduate higher education, unless the latter has traditionally admitted students of only one sex.[5] As a result, Title IX does not apply to admissions to nonvocational elementary or secondary schools, nor does it apply to certain institutions of undergraduate higher education. This means that Title IX permits public or private single-sex elementary and secondary schools, as well as some single-sex colleges.

This exception for single-sex schools has existed since the legislation was enacted, and "the legislative history indicates that Congress excepted elementary and secondary schools from Title IX because of the potential benefits of single-sex education."[6] Less clear is whether Congress intended to permit coeducational schools to establish individual classes on a single-sex basis, as ED's regulations now allow.

THE 2006 REGULATIONS

Noting that some studies demonstrate that students learn better in a single-sex educational environment, ED issued new Title IX regulations in 2006 that provide recipients of educational funding with additional flexibility in providing single-sex classes.[7] The regulations apply to both public and private elementary and secondary schools but not to vocational schools. Specifically, the regulations permit recipients to offer single-sex classes and extracurricular activities "if (1) the purpose of the class or extracurricular activity is achievement of an important governmental or educational objective, and (2) the single-sex nature of the class or extracurricular activity is substantially related to achievement of that objective."[8] In its regulations, ED identified two objectives that would meet the first requirement: (1) to provide a diversity of educational options to parents and students, and (2) to meet the particular, identified educational needs of students.

According to the regulations, any schools that choose to provide single-sex classes must meet certain requirements designed to ensure nondiscrimination. For example, participation in single-sex classes must be completely voluntary, recipients must treat male and female students in an "evenhanded" manner, and a recipient's justification must be genuine. These latter requirements mean than a school's use of overly broad sex-based generalizations in connection with offering single-sex education would be sex discrimination. Thus, recipients are prohibited from providing single-sex classes on the basis of generalizations about the different talents, capacities, or preferences of either sex.

In addition, although schools must always provide a "substantially equal" coeducational class in the same subject, they are not always required to provide single-sex classes for the excluded sex, unless such classes would be required to ensure nondiscriminatory implementation. If recipients can show that students of the excluded sex are not interested in enrolling in a single-sex class or do not have educational needs that can be addressed by such a class, then they are not required to offer a corresponding single-sex class to the excluded sex. Although schools must offer classes that are substantially equal, these classes do not have to be identical. In comparing classes under the "substantially equal" requirement, ED will consider a range of factors, including, but not limited to, admissions policies; the educational benefits provided, including the quality, range, and content of curriculum and other services, and the quality and availability of books, instructional materials, and technology; the qualifications of faculty and staff; the quality, accessibility, and availability of facilities and resources; geographic accessibility; and intangible features, such as the reputation of the faculty.

In order to ensure compliance with the regulations, recipients are required to periodically conduct self-evaluations, and students or their parents who believe the regulations have been violated may file a complaint with the school or with ED. ED also has the authority to conduct periodic compliance reviews. According to the National Association for Single Sex Public Education, there are currently at least 514 public schools in the United States that offer single-sex education in the form of single-sex schools or classrooms.[9]

STATUTORY IMPLICATIONS

As noted above, the enactment of the new regulations raises questions regarding whether ED has the statutory authority under Title IX to authorize single-sex classrooms and whether the regulations comply with the statutory requirements of the EEOA.

Title IX

Although Title IX explicitly authorizes single-sex schools, the statute is silent with respect to the question of single-sex classrooms within schools that are otherwise coeducational. As a result, it is possible that the regulations could face a legal challenge on the grounds that ED exceeded its statutory authority. Any court ruling as to the validity of ED's regulations would hinge on the level of deference paid to the agency decision by the reviewing court. The standard for judicial review of such agency action was delineated in *Chevron U.S.A. Inc. v. Natural Resources Defense Council.*[10] There, the Supreme Court established that judicial review of an agency's interpretation of a statute consists of two related questions. First, the court must determine whether Congress has spoken directly to the precise issue at hand. If the intent of Congress is clear, the inquiry is concluded, since the unambiguously expressed intent of Congress must be respected.[11] However, if the court determines that the statute is silent or ambiguous with respect to the specific issue at hand, the court must determine "whether the agency's answer is based on a permissible construction of the statute."[12]

It is important to note that the second prong does not require a court to "conclude that the agency construction was the only one it permissibly could have adopted to uphold the construction, or even the reading the court would have reached if the question initially had arisen in a judicial proceeding."[13] The practical effect of this maxim is that a reasonable agency interpretation of an ambiguous statute must be accorded deference, even if the court believes the agency is incorrect.[14] Ultimately, given Title IX's silence with respect to single-sex classrooms, it's possible, but not certain, that a court could determine that the statutory language was ambiguous enough to support ED's interpretation of the statute.

Equal Educational Opportunity Act

Although the EEOA contains a congressional finding that "the maintenance of dual school systems in which students are assigned to schools solely on the basis of race, color, sex, or national origin denies to those students the equal protection of the laws guaranteed by the fourteenth amendment,"[15] the statute's prohibition against "the deliberate segregation" of students applies only to segregation on the basis of race, color, or national origin, but not sex.[16] Therefore, ED's regulations regarding single-sex classrooms do not appear to conflict with the EEOA.

Over the years, several courts have considered the question of whether single-sex education violates the EEOA. Although these cases, which are few in number, have contemplated single-sex schools rather than single-sex classes, they are instructive. For example, in *Vorchheimer v. School District of Philadelphia*,[17] the Court of Appeals for the Third Circuit considered a challenge filed by a female student who was denied admission to an all-male public high school in Philadelphia. Because the statute did not explicitly prohibit the segregation of schools by sex and because the corresponding all-female high school was found to provide equal educational opportunities for girls, the court rejected the EEOA challenge.

In *United States v. Hinds County School Board*,[18] however, the Fifth Circuit held that the EEOA prohibited a Mississippi school district from splitting the four schools in the district into two all-male schools and two-all female schools.

The court distinguished the case from the *Vorchheimer* decision, noting that *Vorchheimer* involved two voluntary single-sex schools in an otherwise coeducational school system while the Mississippi school district in question involved the mandatory sex segregation of all of the schools, and therefore all of the students, in the system. Read together, these cases indicate that the EEOA may permit single-sex schools as long as coeducational options are available. Such an interpretation would mean that the new Title IX regulatory requirements are consistent with the EEOA.

CONSTITUTIONAL IMPLICATIONS

As noted above, the 2006 Title IX regulations may raise constitutional issues for public schools that offer single-sex classes. Under the equal protection clause of the Fourteenth Amendment,[19] which prohibits the government from denying to any individual the equal protection of the law, governmental classifications that are based on sex receive heightened scrutiny from the courts. Laws that rely on sex-based classifications will survive such scrutiny only if they are substantially related to achieving an important government objective.[20]

Currently, there are only two Supreme Court cases that address the equal protection implications of sex-segregated schools. Although both of these cases occurred in a higher education setting, they provide some guidance that may be applicable to the elementary and secondary education context. In the earlier case, *Mississippi University for Women v. Hogan*,[21] the Court held that the exclusion of an individual from a publicly funded school because of his or her sex violates the equal protection clause unless the government can show that the sex-based classification serves important governmental objectives and that the discriminatory means employed are substantially related to the achievement of those objectives. Because the Court found that the state had not met this burden, it struck down Mississippi's policy of excluding men from its state-supported nursing school for women.

The Court's most recent constitutional pronouncement with respect to sex discrimination in education occurred in *United States v. Virginia*.[22] In that case, the Court held that the exclusion of women from the Virginia Military Institute (VMI), a public institution of higher education designed to prepare men for military and civilian leadership, was unconstitutional, despite the fact that the state had created a parallel school for women. Although the Court reiterated that sex-based classifications must be substantially related to an important government interest, the Court also appeared to conduct a more searching form of inquiry by requiring the state to establish an "exceedingly persuasive justification" for its actions.[23] According to the Court, this justification must be genuine and must not rely on overbroad generalizations about the talents, capacities, or preferences of men and women. In applying this standard, the Court rejected the two arguments that Virginia advanced in support of VMI's exclusion of women, namely, that the single-sex education offered by VMI contributed to a diversity of educational approaches in Virginia and that VMI employed a unique method of training that would be destroyed if women were admitted.

In rejecting VMI's first argument, the Court concluded that VMI had not been established or maintained to promote educational diversity. In fact, VMI's "historic and constant plan" was to offer a unique educational benefit to only men,[24] rather than to complement other Virginia institutions by providing a single-sex educational option. With respect to Virginia's second argument, the Court expressed concern over the exclusion of women from VMI because of generalizations about their ability. While the Court believed that VMI's method of instruction did promote important goals, it concluded that the exclusion of women was not substantially related to achieving those goals. After determining that VMI's exclusion of women violated constitutional equal protection requirements, the Court reviewed the state's remedy, a separate school for women known as the Virginia Women's Institute for Leadership (VWIL). Unlike VMI, VWIL did not use an adversarial method of instruction because it was believed to be inappropriate for most women,[25] and VWIL lacked the faculty, facilities, and course offerings available at VMI. Because VWIL was not a comparable single-sex institution for women, the Court concluded that it was an inadequate remedy for the state's equal protection violations, and VMI subsequently became coeducational.

In light of the VMI case, it appears that schools that establish single-sex classrooms under ED's Title IX regulations may face some legal hurdles but are not necessarily constitutionally barred from establishing such classes. Consistent with the Court's ruling, the Title IX regulations require schools that wish to establish single-sex classes to demonstrate that such classes serve an important governmental objective and are substantially related to achievement of that objective. What is unclear is whether the objectives approved by the Title IX regulations—to provide a diversity of educational options to parents and students and to meet the particular, identified educational needs of students—would be sufficiently "important" to pass judicial review.

Although the *Virginia* Court rejected VMI's diversity rationale, it did so because it found that VMI's justification was not genuine. As a result, the Court has not ruled on whether diversity is an important governmental objective in cases involving sex-based classifications, although the Court, which stated in the VMI case that it does not question "the State's prerogative evenhandedly to support diverse educational opportunities," may be inclined to uphold the diversity rationale with regard to the new Title IX regulations.[26] Moreover, the *Virginia* Court ruled that the parallel school Virginia established for women—VWIL—was not a sufficient remedy for the exclusion of women from VMI because it lacked the faculty, facilities, and course offerings available at VMI. In contrast, the Title IX regulations require schools that offer single-sex classes to provide "substantially equal" classes to the excluded sex. While it's not clear whether the Court would view the "substantially equal" requirement as sufficient to pass constitutional muster, judicial resolution in a given case would most likely depend on the specific facts surrounding a school's single-sex class offerings.

Indeed, organizations such as the American Civil Liberties Union (ACLU) regularly file lawsuits against schools that provide single-sex education.[27] For example, the ACLU has filed a lawsuit alleging that single-sex classrooms in Breckenridge County, KY violate the Constitution, Title IX, the EEOA, and state antidiscrimination law and that ED's Title IX regulations violate the Constitution, Title IX, and the Administrative Procedures Act.[28]

End Notes

[1] 20 U.S.C. §§ 1681 et seq.

[2] 71 FR 62530. An explanation of the requirements that were in place before the new regulations were issued is available at 67 FR 31102.

[3] 20 U.S.C. §§ 1701 et seq.

[4] *Id.* at § 1681(a).

[5] *Id.* at §§ 1681(a)(1), (a)(5).

[6] William N. Eskridge, Jr. & Nan D. Hunter, SEXUALITY, GENDER, AND THE LAW 646 (1997).

[7] The regulations also apply to single-sex extracurricular activities, but do not affect athletic requirements under Title IX.

[8] 71 FR 62530.

[9] National Association for Single Sex Public Education, *FAQs*, http://www.singlesexschools.org/home-faq.htm.

[10] 467 U.S. 837 (1984).

[11] *Id.* at 842-43.

[12] *Id.* at 843.

[13] *Id.* at 843, n. 11.

[14] *Id.* at 845.

[15] 20 U.S.C. § 1702.

[16] *Id.* at § 1703(a).

[17] 532 F.2d 880 (3d Cir. 1976), aff'd by an equally divided Court, 430 U.S. 703 (1977). The Third Circuit also upheld the single-sex schools against a constitutional equal protection challenge.

[18] 560 F.2d 619 (5th Cir.-OLD 1977).

[19] U.S. Const. amend. V; U.S. Const. amend. XIV, § 1. The equal protection clause does not apply to private schools.

[20] Craig v. Boren, 429 U.S. 190, 197 (1976).

[21] 458 U.S. 718 (1982).

[22] 518 U.S. 515 (1996).

[23] *Id* at 533.

[24] *Id.* at 540.

[25] *Id.* at 549.

[26] *Id.* at 534, n. 7. See also, id. at 535 ("Single-sex education affords pedagogical benefits to at least some students ... " and "it is not disputed that diversity among public educational institutions can serve the public good.") Notably, the Court has also upheld racial diversity as an important goal in a recent education case. Grutter v. Bollinger, 539 U.S. 306 (U.S. 2003). However, the Court has never decided whether the "particular identified educational needs" objective is an important governmental goal for purposes of justifying sex-based classifications.

[27] Stephanie Weiss, *Sex and Scholarship; Across the Country, Educators Are Asking if Boys, Girls, and Learning Don't Mix,* Wash. Post, July 21, 2002, at W18.

[28] American Civil Liberties Union, "ACLU Represents Students in Challenge to Sex Segregation in Kentucky Public School," press release, May 19, 2008, http://www.aclu.org/womens rights/edu/35391prs20080519.html.

INDEX

D

E

F

S